This is
ALCOHOL

Printed and bound in the UK by MPG Books, Bodmin

Published by Sanctuary Publishing Limited, Sanctuary House, 45-53 Sinclair Road, London W14 0NS, United Kingdom

www.sanctuarypublishing.com

Photo credits in order of appearance: 1. Getty Images Inc 2. Peter Menzel/Science Photo Library 3. Prof K Seddon & Dr T Evans/Queen's University, Belfast/Science Photo Library 4. Science Photo Library 5. George Bernard/Science Photo Library 6. Getty Images Inc 7-9. National Library of Medicine/Science Photo Library 10. George Bernard/Science Photo Library 11-20. Getty Images Inc 21. PA Photos 22. Erika Craddock/Science Photo Library 23. Jim Varney/Science Photo Library 24. Brian Evans/Science Photo Library 25. Science Photo Library 26. Biophoto Associates/Science Photo Library 27. Simon Fraser/Freeman Hospital, Newcastle Upon Tyne/Science Photo Library 28. Pascal Goetgheluck/Science Photo Library 29. Leonard Lessin/Peter Arnold Inc/Science Photo Library 30. PA Photos 31. David Swindells/PYMCA

ISBN: 1-86074-422-2

This is
ALCOHOL

NICK BROWNLEE

CONTENTS

INTRODUCTION

'Alcohol is the anaesthesia by which we endure the operation of life.'
- George Bernard Shaw (1856-1950)

If you were to drink alcohol in its natural, raw state the chances are you would be dead long before you'd even decided you didn't like it. That is because alcohol is a potent chemical that is used in, among other things, anti-freeze and glue.

But when any of us drink wine, beer, champagne, whisky, alcopops, cider, extra-strength lager, absinthe or any of the thousands of variations on the same theme, alcohol becomes a substance that defines us, as well as our culture, our nationality, our beliefs and our social standing. More importantly, we are never drinking alone. Over 85 per cent of all adults drink alcohol. Alcohol is *the* global currency, transcending barriers of language, nationality and culture. It is tempting to think that this is a good thing. The invitation to sit and have a drink, for example, is a symbol of friendship understood the world over, as this example shows:

'I was on holiday, wandering round this market in Istanbul, looking at the rugs and not understanding a word that was being said: typical Brit abroad,' said Colin Dixon, a 33-year-old street trader from Bow, East London. 'Then all of a sudden one of the merchants - a real old guy with a weathered face - waves me over to this little table at the side of his stall. He's got two small glasses and this bottle of raki. He pours us both a drink. Christ, the stuff's like rocket fuel but it did the trick. Half an hour later, the two of us are jabbering away and laughing - not understanding a word of what we're saying, mind you, but at the same time both of us knowing what we were on about. By the end of the afternoon, he's introducing his family! It was magic!'

Magic indeed. Even the Royal College of Psychiatrists, in their 1987 report *Alcohol: Our Favourite Drug*, were moved to pronounce, 'After a few drinks conversation appears to sparkle, dull people seem more interesting and feeble jokes funny'. Alcohol is a proven psychoactive substance that alters minds and moods, can break ice and also remove inhibitions. But before we hug ourselves and dream of international friendships forged over a glass or two of raki, it is worth remembering that the word alcohol itself, as well as the critical process of distilling, came from the Middle East – a part of the world where it is now officially banned and partakers are severely punished. Let us not forget either, that alcohol was so demonized in the United States in the 1920s that it was banned altogether.

> The term 'proof' originated from early days when testing the alcohol content of a whisky used in barter was to mix it with gunpowder to see if it contained enough alcohol to burn. If a clear blue flame resulted from mixing equal parts of gunpowder and whisky, there was proof that the beverage was made up of at least 50 per cent alcohol.

For all its benefits, alcohol never lets us forget that it is a poison and that, like shares, the mood swings it brings on can go down as well as up: 'They were a little drunk when they got to the bar at 10:30am, and they proceeded to drink litres of strong beer well into the afternoon. At first, they were just high-spirited – but then the chanting started. Then a group of Germans came into the square and all hell broke loose. Glass was shattered, furniture smashed. It was as if war had begun.' Those are the words of a barman in Charleroi, Belgium after gangs of English and German football supporters started a drink-fuelled mass brawl during soccer's European Championship finals in 2000.

Excessive alcohol consumption, particularly among the young, is routinely blamed for the rise in violent crime. In 1997, crime linked to alcohol was registered at 350,700 cases in England and Wales alone – that's more than eight per cent of all crime occurring in the British Isles. And yet, despite the impression that football hooligans and violent criminals may give, the British, in general, now drink less than they ever did. Britain's total *per capita* intake of all forms of alcohol is roughly half that of France and Portugal (around 19 pints of pure alcohol per person per year compared to 37 pints) and less than the USA, Australia and New Zealand (all around 23 pints).

This book aims to take an objective view of alcohol in all its manifestations. Firstly, the culture of alcohol around the world is examined to reveal how, in many cases, it has played a defining role in shaping nations. The history of alcohol is also covered. This takes a journey from the time it was first discovered through the years when it changed from being a staple of most of the world's diet to becoming an uncontrolled epidemic, and right up to the present day, in which it has the power to determine policies and dictate lives.

This books also explains exactly what alcohol is and what effects it has on those who drink it; for example why it has the capacity to give some people great enjoyment and yet leave others in abject misery. The different ways that alcohol is regarded and consumed around the world are revealed too, along with how certain types of alcohol have developed to meet the needs and tastes of people from all corners of the globe. Finally, the sheer power of alcohol in modern society is discussed in detail because it has now become an industry to rival any in the modern world.

Throughout the research for this book I have talked to ordinary people as well as so-called experts in order to gain a full picture of alcohol in the 21st century. Whether you drink or not, and whether you know it or not, alcohol is a subject that affects your life in some way. This book will show you why.

01

CULTURE

'Let us have wine and women, mirth and laughter. Sermons and soda water the day after.' - Lord Byron (1788-1824)

ALCOHOL: THE DRUG OF CHOICE

The photograph was as horrifying as it was graphic: a young girl curled up on her bedroom floor, her limbs bloated and mottled by death, an empty syringe lying on the carpet beside her.

The image of 21-year-old heroin addict Rachel Whitear, released to the public domain by her grieving parents as a warning to other young people, was accompanied by screaming headlines about how the narcotic was a deadly threat to Britain's youth. It bore striking similarities to the deathbed photographs of Leah Betts, the teenager who died after taking an Ecstasy tablet at a nightclub - and both tragedies sat well with opponents of cannabis, a drug that, after decades of prohibition, had just been declassified to the same level as sleeping pills and was well on the way to being decriminalized for medical use. It may be a 'soft drug' they argued, but it remained a gateway to the kind of hard stuff that killed Rachel and Leah.

Yet even as society railed at the seemingly unchecked rise of the drugs menace, the most widely available and potentially damaging drug of all went largely unnoticed - a drug that has killed 20 times more teenagers in the last 10 years than heroin or Ecstasy and is responsible annually for almost 2 million deaths worldwide. In terms of statistics, it should be classified right up there with the worst of them. But then no drug has ever insinuated itself so effectively into the fabric of human culture as alcohol.

It may have killed millions and acquired names such as 'the demon drink' and 'mother's ruin' during its long and chequered history, but by and large the world takes a pretty relaxed view about booze. After all, it is an integral part of our lives: our births are traditionally celebrated with it, we grow up watching our parents consuming it and we wait impatiently until the day when we can legally consume it ourselves. As adults we spend much of our time in places where alcohol is served, and a substantial amount of our annual salary is set aside to purchase it. We drink it at marriage ceremonies and at funeral wakes. We see it advertised every day on television, in newspapers and on billboards; we attend sporting events sponsored by alcohol manufacturers. We give it as gifts to loved ones, and toast their health with it. We take it to parties and drink it to break the ice. We go on trips to see where it is produced. Our most creative talents swear by it. Protestants, Roman Catholics and Jews sanction it.

Yet the same stuff makes us incontinent and incomprehensible. It leaves us bankrupt and unemployed. We wake with thumping headaches after drinking it and vow never to drink it again. We watch our children like hawks and smell their breath when they come in from parties. Twice as many marriages end in divorce through alcohol than through adultery. The people on the adverts don't have red eyes, beer bellies, bad breath and cirrhosis of the liver; our sporting heroes might wear a brand name on their shirt, but they don't drink the product because it has been proved to destroy their fitness – those that do drink are now shambling wrecks of their former selves. At parties we drink too much, say things we don't mean and sleep with people we don't know. We can't drive anywhere after drinking because if we're caught it can mean a jail sentence, yet anybody who drinks shandy down the pub is seen as weak.

> Airlines and their long-suffering customers are reporting a steep climb in air-rage incidents, most of them drink related. Not surprisingly, given its huge aviation industry, a large proportion of the high-altitude incidents take place on flights within and from the USA.

If this sounds like a classic state of schizophrenia, then it is no coincidence. Unlike with other drugs, society's relationship with alcohol is complex and ill-defined. There are few apologists for heroin, other than the most hardened addict, while cannabis users remain in the minority and cocaine and Ecstasy users make up a tiny percentage of the population. But almost everyone uses alcohol – young, old, rich, poor; even people who run centres to treat alcohol abuse enjoy a tipple.

We feel horror when we see photographs of young people such as Rachel Whitear and Leah Betts, and we campaign vociferously for drugs to be banned, and vilify traffickers and pushers. Yet when someone drinks themselves to death, or publicly admits they are a helpless alcoholic it is regarded as just one of those things. Even when the media horror-show turns its attention to subjects like under-age drinking fatalities, our reaction is to shrug our shoulders and go to the pub.

Why should this be? Wine writer Jancis Robinson notes, 'It is the dogmatism with which we insist that to drink is normal, to abstain abnormal, that suggests our attitudes to alcohol are not quite as relaxed as they seem. The reason we do not take the trouble to scrutinize our drinking habits may be partly because we are reluctant about what that scrutiny might reveal.'

WHERE WE DRINK – SPIT-AND-SAWDUST TO EUROBARS

The English city of Newcastle-upon-Tyne is famous for its football team, for the team's star striker Alan Shearer and for the iron and steel starburst of the bridge that spans the river. Its recent history also provides a graphic illustration of how drinking culture has changed – not just in this corner of northeast England but in the whole of Britain, and indeed Europe, over the last 40 years.

West of the city, hugging the north bank of the Tyne, is Scotswood Road. It was built in the 1850s to house workers from the huge Armstrong's armaments factories, which stretched for 5km from Scotswood to Elswick. By the turn of the century the workforce had reached around 2,000. On one side of Scotswood Road were the sprawling factories that employed the labourers from the seemingly endless rows of terraced housing on the

Gathering grapes in a vineyard at Pommard, near Beaune, in the Cote D'Or district of Burgundy.

Hundreds of wooden wine barrels stacked in rows in a vineyard warehouse. Red wine is matured in wooden barrels for 3-4 years before being bottled to improve and soften its flavour. Air passes very slowly through the wood, encouraging the formation of complex esters, produced when acid and alcohol react together in the wine. The aromatic esters give the wine its distinctive flavour and smell. At the same time, the levels of tannin (the bitter principle from the grape skin in red wine) and acid fall, making the wine smoother and less tart. Subtle flavours may also be absorbed from the wood, sometimes giving a smoky quality.

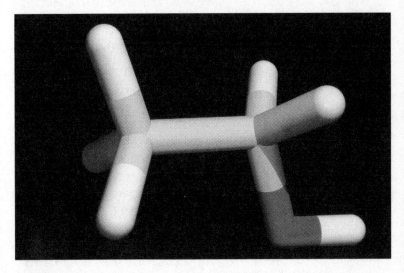

Computer illustration of a molecule of ethanol, or alcohol (formula C_2H_5OH), with the atoms represented as cylinders. Ethanol is widely used as a solvent in industry and in laboratories, but its main use is in alcoholic drinks. Taken in moderation, ethanol removes a drinker's inhibitions and gives a sense of confidence, while larger doses lead to a lack of co-ordination and even death. It is addictive with prolonged heavy use.

other side. And at the end of each terrace there was a pub – well, 56 of them to be precise.

The pubs sprang up to service the needs of the labourers, to be places away from the strictures of the workplace where as well as drinking and socializing they could hold union meetings and discuss the issues of the day as they affected them. Many became synonymous with the various trades that worked in the factories across the road. They were not pubs as we would recognize them today. They were uniformly drab, smoke-filled establishments and restricted to men only – apart from the landlady – but that was how the drinkers liked it. They were also social centres, around which the community revolved; if there was a family problem to be solved, it was solved over a few pints.

Today, there are just two pubs left on Scotswood Road. The rest were bulldozed along with the terraces, as was much of the industry that once sustained them. Those people that remain do not remember the community spirit of the terraces. They certainly don't remember the pubs – and in any case the idea of drinking in the same boozers as their dads is a non-starter. For them, the bright lights and bars of the city centre are just a short bus ride away.

'I live in Scotswood, but there's no way I would drink there,' says 19-year-old Darren Roberts. 'The pubs are boring. Shit. Full of old gadgies. Everyone goes into the town on a Friday and Saturday night, hits the bars.'

It was in the town centre that, during the 1980s, Tyneside drinking culture dragged itself out of the doldrums in which it had wallowed for years and set a benchmark for the rest of the country. On the back of Thatcherite capitalism, new money was pumped into the city by rich young businessmen who a generation earlier would have earned their money like everyone else down the pits or in the shipyards. The dingy old pubs were gutted and reopened as sparkling new designer bars with names like Masters, Presidents and Ricks. Brown Ale and Best Scotch bitter were replaced by Red Stripe and Becks. And the hard core of flat-capped, ageing drinkers were usurped by young men and women who were happy to wear short-sleeved shirts and short skirts even in the icy cold of a northeast winter.

After the success of this venture, developers quickly moved to transform run-down city centre pubs in places like Bristol, Manchester and Leeds into money-spinning bars. Others bought up once grand but now derelict premises formerly occupied by banks and shops and turned them into vast, marble-floored venues for young people to meet and drink in.

The effect on drinking culture on a wider scale was electric. Suddenly brewers began looking with jaundiced eyes on the pubs that had traditionally provided the backbone of their business. Almost overnight the old-fashioned British boozer, with its mouldy cheese sandwiches, dart boards and dominoes boards was not only outdated, but massively unprofitable compared to the city-centre bars packed to the rafters with kids with expendable incomes. In the early 1970s, there had been an abortive attempt to change drinking habits when the brewers replaced hand-pulled ale with long-life keg fizz. But the outcry, coupled with the fact that keg fizz was disgusting, had given tradition a stay of execution. Now, however, there was to be no mercy. As older drinkers looked on in despair, their local pub was either sold or else turned into a 'theme' pub, complete with continental lager, plastic palm trees and brass-effect railings, in an attempt to replicate the city bars.

Yet by the mid-1990s, even the days of these brash, lively theme bars were numbered as the marketing men identified a new type of drinker who needed catering for: women. The expensive steel and glass developments that were rapidly replacing the dingy pubs provided the perfect location for a new breed of bar – one that was light, airy, served a range of tasty food and wine and which actively courted young professional women with money in their pockets. The existing bars along the quayside swiftly followed suit, ripping out the brass and the palm trees and replacing them with designer furniture and pastel shades. As a result, Friday and Saturday nights were still packed out, but now increasing numbers of people – particularly groups of women – were choosing to go out to eat and drink during the week. The revolution was complete. In the space of just a few years, the drinking culture of generations had been turned on its head.

The UK is merely the highest-profile casualty of a Europe-wide homogenization of drinking culture. If you had gone to a bar in Paris, Rome, Barcelona or any other major city on the continent 20 or 30 years ago, you would have found distinct differences in service, alcohol, atmosphere and clientele, just as you would have had you gone to Newcastle or London. Go to any of these places today and you'll get the same look, the same beer and the same thumping soundtrack wherever you are. In Bologna, a city famed for its diversity of food and drink, the bar that most young people frequent is an Irish theme pub that serves ice-cold Guinness and plates of chips. In Lisbon, the beer pumps dispense Whitbread Smoothflow along with Budweiser, Hoegarten, San Miguel and Peroni. Ask for traditional Italian or Portuguese beverages, and you'll most likely be directed to the nearest tourist shop.

'In Spain, the young people like to party. It is the same around the rest of Europe,' says Alicia Hernandez, a student from Madrid. 'I have friends who come from Britain, from Italy, from Germany and we all like the same thing. Europe is no longer a place of different countries. Is it a shame? Maybe – but it is progress.'

You can take your pick of what to blame – if blame is indeed the right word – for this alcohol monoculturalism: increased European travel, satellite TV, pop music... It makes little difference in the long run. When it comes to where we drink, Europe has defied the sceptics by uniting as one. And while the seemingly genetic need of the British and Scandinavians to drink copious amounts of beer (and of the French and the Italians to consume wine by the gallon) until they are incapacitated will never fade away, drinking has become more cosmopolitan. The new generation of drinkers are more choosy about where and what they drink and who they drink with – and it is they that are dictating the market rather than the other way around.

'TIME GENTLEMEN, PLEASE' – LICENSING LAWS AND THE 'LAST ORDERS' CULTURE

For English football fans, qualification for the 2002 World Cup Finals was a mixed blessing. No sooner had David Beckham's screaming last-minute free kick bulged the net against the Greeks to assure England's safe passage, than the more prosaic fans were pointing out the problems involved.

'We were all in the pub getting pissed after the Greece game, when someone says, "Hang on, it's bloody Japan and Korea, isn't it?" ' recalls fervent England fan Lawrence Parker. '"So what?" we says. "Well it's the time difference, innit? They're going to be kicking off every match first thing in the morning UK time." We asked the landlord of the pub if he was going to be showing the games and he just shook his head, saying it was against the law. We couldn't believe it! All that bother getting through to the World Cup and you've got to watch the team in your pyjamas with a cup of tea. How gutting is that?'

The landlord was right. A series of legal decisions in the 1970s and 1980s meant that, in effect, landlords were banned from opening at abnormal hours. One case of particular relevance was in 1978 when magistrates in Leicester rejected an appeal for pubs to open during matches in the Argentina World Cup Finals on the grounds that fans watching on pub televisions were not 'participants in the game'.

But for Lawrence Parker and his pals, salvation was at hand thanks to a determined pub landlord from Bristol called Martin Gough. In April 2002, Mr Gough was so incensed by the decision of magistrates in the city to refuse permission for him to serve beer during England's early-morning games, that he took the case to the High Court. There, Lord Woolf, the Lord Chief Justice, granted an order of special exemption allowing Mr Gough to open, paving the way for pubs across the UK to open their doors at breakfast time. He reminded justices that the current licensing laws allowed granting of special exemptions for customers to participate in genuine special occasions, which were not just an excuse for landlords to serve more alcohol.

Dismissing previous rulings as outdated, Lord Woolf said, 'If one were to ask anyone today whether the World Cup was a national special event, I apprehend that the reaction would be immediate that it was just such an event. The customers are going to the public house... to take part in a collective enjoyment of the event.' Lord Woolf also said that watching football on a giant screen in a pub had become an 'acknowledged leisure event'.

But while the decision meant early mornings for publicans and an unprecedented number of 'sickies' phoned in on the day of England matches, it had little effect on Britain's antiquated licensing laws and the ongoing saga about whether they should be updated.

Drinking culture is invariably dominated by the licensing laws of the individual country. And even a cursory glance at the global list reveals that those countries traditionally perceived as having an 'easy-going' attitude towards drink tend to be those with the slackest regulations. In Italy, for example, it is possible to buy a drink at all hours. Indeed, the only restrictions are on the sale of drinks with an alcohol content of over 21 per cent, and that is only at public events. In France, restrictions on hours of sale are more complicated – they are determined by individual local authorities – but there is no restriction on which day and from which outlet you can buy your alcohol. In any case, most French local authorities are quite content to allow the hours of sale to be at the discretion of the individual retailer. It's largely the same story in other southern European countries like Spain, Portugal and Greece.

Conversely, in heavy-drinking Scandinavian countries like Denmark and Sweden, the restrictions are draconian compared to those in France and Italy. The Danes can only buy alcohol until 5:30pm during the week, and until 12 noon on Saturday. There is a blanket ban on advertising on TV and radio, and a strict voluntary code restricts ads in newspapers, magazines, cinemas and on billboards. In Sweden, it is even harder to get a drink: all stores are closed at weekends, and outlets are not allowed in areas where they could be perceived as 'contributing to social problems'. They are also prohibited in the immediate neighbourhood of schools. Strong beer can only be bought in state-run stores. In Norway, meanwhile, as well as similar licensing restrictions, drinking is banned in public places. Even in supposedly 'liberal' Holland it can be harder to get a drink than it is to get a joint. Liquor shops and supermarkets are closed on Sundays and in evenings, while the opening hours of bars and discos are restricted locally by the mayor.

In the UK, the basis of the current restrictions dates back to 1915 when, in order to stop vital war workers turning up drunk for work, pub closing time was set at 11pm. Until the 1990s it was only possible to drink during the week from 11am–3pm and 5:30–11pm, while on Sundays the pubs would only open for a couple of hours at lunchtime. This, of course, put the UK out of step with its European neighbours, where bars and cafés can generally stay open until the owner decides it is time to go to bed. The laws were relaxed slightly in the early 1990s, when it was deemed acceptable for pubs to open all day – providing the landlord wanted to. But the uniform 11pm turfing out time has remained in force. This has annoyed many campaigners, who have pointed out that the increasing culture of binge drinking has had a lot to do with the fact that many drinkers feel obliged to beat the clock by downing as much alcohol as possible in the time allowed to them. The so-called 11 o'clock swill, where drinkers buy and consume vast rounds before the time bell is sounded, is symptomatic of the outdated licensing situation.

> Kinpaku-iri sake, a Japanese rice wine, contains flakes of real gold. While this adds a touch of extravagance, it doesn't affect the flavour at all.

'The whole industry believes it is stupid for someone not to be able to leave the theatre or cinema and have a relaxed drink,' said Rob Hayward of the Brewers and Licensed Retailers Association. 'At the moment you can only get a late license if you want to make a noise – for music, dancing or public entertainment. Why can't people have a late, quiet drink?'

The election of the Labour government in 1997 gave rise to hopes that wholesale changes were on their way. In April 2000, in the run-up to the General Election, Home Secretary Jack Straw once again re-ignited the debate by releasing a White Paper entitled 'Time For Reform', detailing proposals for the laws. Predictably perhaps, Labour won the election but then proved it was they who didn't really give a XXXX for the revamped licensing laws when the proposals were not included in the Queen's speech.

But what difference would it make to British cultural life if 24-hour drinking actually made it onto the statute books? Closing time and the 11 o'clock swill have become ingrained on the drinking public psyche.

'When the last orders bell goes, I've seen people come up to the bar and buy three or four pints just for themselves – even though they've only got 10 minutes to closing time and another 15, or 20 if they're lucky, before we chuck 'em out,' says barmaid Louise Daniels from Chelmsford, Essex. 'Even when the last bell has gone, they'll still try to get served by telling you that they've been waiting for ages and you haven't seen them.'

Of course, the last orders mindset is not simply restricted to the pub.

Image from 1512 of a medieval apothecary using bellows on the furnace of a still to make medicinal spirits. Flasks containing wine were placed in the opening above the furnace. Alcohol, being more volatile than water, would evaporate first and be collected in a flask (RIGHT). Medieval texts claimed that alcohol should be distilled at least seven times before it could be used as medicine. Alcoholic spirits were known as *aqua vitae* ('waters of life'). They were thought to be materialized life-force because, as an antiseptic, they cured infected wounds. Spirits were widely used in medicines and ointments for a variety of illnesses.

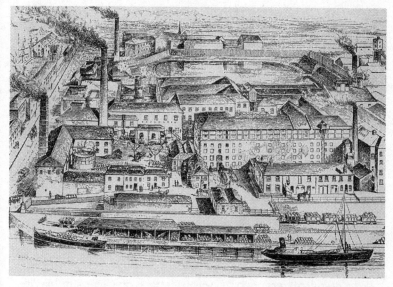

Dundas Hill Whisky Distillery, Glasgow, 1887. Whisky is made by concentrating the alcohol of beer in a still. The liquid is then boiled and the alcohol is sublimed as vapour, then condensed and matured in wooden barrels. The first recorded whisky production in Scotland took place in 1494, but the modern industry dates from the 1820s, when legislation supressed small-scale production in favour of large, licensed distilleries.

Once the pub door has slammed shut for the last time, the night is not necessarily over. Drinkers in Britain spend millions of pounds on post-pub grub – the UK Indian food industry alone is estimated at £2.8 billion ($4.1 billion) a year, with a fifth of that coming from sales after closing time. 'People often ask why we put up with crowds of drunken lads who come into the restaurant after closing time,' says Birmingham restaurateur Asif Khan. 'But business is business and these people are paying customers. Sure, we get the odd ones now and again who try to do a runner, but it is pretty rare. And if they are too drunk, we won't serve them. Even if pubs stay open longer, I can't see it affecting our trade too much because people will always be hungry after a night on the beer. They may come in later, that's all.'

One post-pub tradition that may suffer is the nightclub. 'Later licensing hours for pubs will be the death knell for a lot of clubs,' says veteran club owner Peter Stringfellow. 'There is a trend towards lounging rather than dancing.' Perhaps as a pre-emptive strike, a number of nightclubs that used to open their doors after closing time are now opening earlier and serving food before turning their premises over to late-night discotheques in a bid to snare punters.

CREATIVE DRINKING – ALCOHOL AND THE ARTS
POP STARS

When the autopsy was performed on Keith Moon, drummer with The Who and the self-styled legendary wildman of rock who died in 1978, they discovered that the cause of death was a massive drugs overdose. There were 32 tablets of Heminevrin in his system, 26 of which were undissolved. Heminevrin was the drug prescribed to wean Moon off alcohol, which he consumed in such heroic and varied quantities that doctors warned it would one day kill him. The man who once drove a Rolls Royce into a swimming pool would have appreciated the irony.

Rock 'n' roll is a profession littered with premature deaths from alcohol abuse. Jim Morrison of The Doors died of a heart attack in the bath, his once muscled physique bloated by alcohol. Bon Scott of AC/DC choked on his own vomit after a marathon drinking session, as did Led

Zeppelin drummer John Bonham. Dennis Wilson of The Beach Boys drowned while drunk. Indeed, those grizzled veterans who have survived into middle age tend to view the current generation of squeaky-clean pop idols as somehow betraying the legend they created in their outlandish heyday of the 1960s and 1970s. When the likes of Liam Gallagher of Oasis and Robbie Williams occasionally hit the headlines for their boozing and brawling, it tends to be the exception to the rule. With most pop records now being bought by impressionable eight and nine-year-olds, agents and record company publicists no longer regard it as beneficial to publicize the excesses of their clients as they did when Led Zep, Black Sabbath and AC/DC bestrode planet rock. The term 'rock dinosaur' is overused, but it remains particularly applicable to survivors like Ozzie Osborne, Iggy Pop and Alice Cooper – the latter once boasted, 'I was drinking two quarts of whiskey a day after my three-month treatment in a sanatorium just to keep going.'

The music industry does, by its very nature, tend to expose its miscreants to the full glare of publicity. Moon, Morrison, Wilson and Co may have died young, but they lived and drank in exactly the way we once expected of our rock stars. But it's not just Rock 'n' Roll that enjoys such an affiliation with booze.

WRITERS

While writing *In Cold Blood*, his seminal and ground-breaking study of real-life murder published in 1966, the author Truman Capote liked nothing better to aid the often tortuous creative process than a double martini before lunch. During lunch he would have another double martini and, after it a stinger, a cocktail of brandy and crème de menthe. Capote would then continue to drink steadily throughout the afternoon until he was too drunk to type. Then, most evenings, he would jump in his car and go for a drive around Long Island, where he had one of his two homes.

It took Capote six years and a lot of martini to write *In Cold Blood*. It was only when he was arrested for drunken driving and threatened with a lengthy prison sentence that he decided that his drinking was perhaps becoming a little excessive. He checked into Silver Hill, an expensive clinic in Connecticut where, after several weeks, he was pronounced dry by the counsellors and allowed back home.

Within days, however, Capote not only was smashed again but so were his front teeth and his skull following a spectacular drunken fall. This time, Capote checked into the Smithers Alcoholism Rehabilitation Unit of St Luke's Roosevelt Hospital in New York – an establishment acidly described by the writer as the 'Devil's Island of alcohol clinics'. A few weeks later, dry once again, he checked out. A couple of weeks after that he appeared on a TV chat show so drunk that he could barely speak. The pattern of bingeing and drying out continued to repeat itself until Capote's death from acute liver failure, aged 59, in 1984.

Capote died much the way he had lived, a shambling, helpless alcoholic who caused horrific booze-induced damage to both his body and brain. Capote – once blond, beautiful, and envied – died bald, bloated, and unloved, the precocious talent for observation and reportage that saw him published at just 23 years old diminished to vindictive magazine gossip and crippling writer's block. He was all washed up on a sea of alcoholic excess. And yet, to many, Truman Capote remains the very epitome of what a successful writer should be: someone with rare insight into the human condition, yet damned with a fatal inability to come to terms with their own. Capote's uncontrolled thirst for hard drink, his wild binges, his failed attempts at self-cure and his eventual early death have been seen as being as important as his writing talent. Probably because it all added to the 'glamour'...

Writing and alcohol have always made willing bedfellows, and some of literature's greatest names – Edgar Allan Poe, Stephen Crane, Dylan Thomas, Herman Melville, Dorothy Parker, F Scott Fitzgerald and William Faulkner – were heavy-duty drinkers if not full blown alcoholics. Indeed, in most cases, alcoholism was not simply a consequence of writing, but a vital and self-serving part of the process itself. In his 1913 memoir *John Barleycorn*, Jack London, author of *Call Of The Wild,* recalled how for many years he refused to drink until he had completed his daily 1,000 words. The trouble was, London began rising extra early in order to slap down 1,000 words long before lunch. 'The more I drank, the more I was compelled to drink in order to get an effect,' he wrote. 'I had the craving, and it was mastering me.' London eventually quit drinking aged 37. He committed suicide three years later, unable to come to terms with a dry existence.

Suicide brought on by alcoholic depression in many cases merely hastens the inevitable. Donald W Goodwin, chairman of the Department of Psychiatry at the University of Kansas Medical Centre, and author of *Alcohol And The Writer,* points out that statistically, after publicans, more writers die of cirrhosis of the liver than any other profession. Of the seven American winners of the Nobel Prize for literature, Goodwin observes that four of them - Sinclair Lewis, Eugene O'Neill, William Faulkner and Ernest Hemingway - were confirmed alcoholics, while a fifth, John Steinbeck, drank to excess. 'Writers make their own hours, so it is easier for them to drink,' he says. 'It is expected that writers will drink and writers live up to the expectation.' This was certainly true of writers such as Brendan Behan, Raymond Carver, Dylan Thomas and John Cheever, who embraced alcohol abuse and its consequences as enthusiastically as they wrote about it.

In a profession littered with heroic drinkers, the daddy of them all was without doubt Ernest Hemingway. A typical day's consumption for the author of such classics as *The Old Man And The Sea, The Sun Also Rises* and *For Whom The Bell Tolls* would begin with a breakfast of tea and gin followed by regular shots of absinthe, whisky and vodka. Lunch would consist of three or four large martinis washed down with five or six bottles of wine. 'Papa' claimed it helped him write. His drinking exploits certainly contributed to his image as a macho man's man. Unfortunately, they also contributed to hypertension, kidney and liver disease, oedema of the ankles, high blood urea, mild diabetes, haemachromatosis, recurrent muscle cramps, chronic sleeplessness and sexual impotence. His alcoholism would have undoubtedly killed him, had he not blown his own brains out in a fit of depression at the age of 62.

Of course, not every great writer was/is an alcoholic. Mark Twain, Edith Wharton, Tom Wolfe and Emily Dickinson, to name just four, have all been responsible for literary masterpieces without resorting to gin with their breakfast cuppa. Others, such as John Cheever, successfully conquered their alcoholism and went on to produce some of their finest work. 'It wasn't just that he didn't drink any more... it was like having my father back,' Cheever's daughter Susan wrote in her memoir *Home Before Dark*. 'He went from being an alcoholic with a drug problem who smoked two packs of Marlboros a day to being a man so abstemious that his principal drugs were the sugar in his desserts and the caffeine in the tea that he drank instead of whisky.' A year after checking out of the alcohol clinic Cheever finished *Falconer*, his most successful novel.

Despite this, the link between alcohol and writers remains as tangible as ever. John Cheever was once a member of the Iowa Writers' Workshop, which also included such literary luminaries as Philip Roth and Kurt Vonnegut. In 1987, a 15-year study of 30 creative writers attached to the Workshop found that 30 per cent of them were alcoholics, compared with 7 per cent in the comparison group of non-writers.

ACTORS

The movie industry has a similarly profound relationship with alcohol. In the Oscar-winning movie *Leaving Las Vegas*, Nicolas Cage plays a full-blown alcoholic who loses his job and decides to move to Las Vegas, sell all of his possessions and drink himself to death. It's moving stuff, especially when Cage meets a hooker with a heart of gold who nursemaids him through his final days. Critics praised the film for its uncompromising approach to a difficult subject, and compared it to the 1945 classic *The Lost Weekend*, in which Ray Milland plays a booze-sodden writer who deals with his inability to begin his novel by going on an epic bender. Both films deal squarely with the deleterious effects of alcohol not only on the user, but on those who love him. They leave the audience sympathizing with the anti-hero, and at the same time recoiling at the squalor in which he finds himself as a result of drinking.

But while Hollywood may like to portray itself as a moral arbiter, showing us the seedy underbelly of booze culture, the reality is greatly different. Like an alcoholic doctor, Hollywood feels duty bound to warn us of the effects of drink while keeping a quart of bourbon in its desk drawer.

Between 1996 and 1997 – a year before *Leaving Las Vegas* was released – the Office of National Drug Control Policy (ONDCP) and the US Department of Health and Human Services conducted a $400,000 (£272,000) survey of 200 of that year's most popular movie rentals. The purpose of the survey was to gauge the extent to which the use of alcohol, tobacco or illegal drugs were depicted by film makers, and the movies surveyed were as diverse as *Get Shorty*, *Casino*, *The Usual Suspects*, *Operation Dumbo Drop*, *Toy Story*, and *Dunston Checks In*.

The survey found that, while illicit drug use was depicted in 22 per cent of movies and tobacco use in 89 per cent, a whopping 93 per cent of the movies surveyed depicted the use of alcohol. In other words, despite movies such as *Leaving Las Vegas* and *The Lost Weekend* preaching the evils of drink, alcohol was revealed to be an integral part of both plot and characterization in most Hollywood movies.

The report concluded, 'In both television and film, alcoholic beverages are more likely to be consumed than non-alcoholic beverages. Drinkers...tend to be leading characters, often protagonists, and usually successful.'

Meanwhile General Barry McCaffrey, director of ONDCP, urged the entertainment industry to tie depictions of drug use to addictive behaviour and negative consequences. 'Entertainment should depict drugs as unglamorous, dangerous and socially unacceptable, and drug use should not be portrayed as humorous,' he said.

But should we be surprised at Hollywood's apparent fixation with drink? Film makers would argue that alcohol is such a part of western society that to deliberately censor it, or portray everyone who has a drink as a socially unacceptable loser, would make the movies a laughing stock. What's more, it would lay the film industry open to accusations of gross hypocrisy. Actors, after all, have never been averse to a drink...

On 1 May 1999, the British actor Oliver Reed entered a bar in Malta and ordered a beer. Reed was in good spirits: the reason he was in Malta was because he had landed the plum role of Proximo the gladiator trainer in the movie *Gladiator*, which was being filmed on the island. It is estimated that on that warm May day in Valletta, Reed drank a dozen or so strong beers before moving onto a prolonged bout of arm-wrestling and brandy drinking with some Maltese friends and a group of sailors from the frigate HMS *Cumberland*, which happened to be moored in the harbour. As the afternoon dragged on, Reed suddenly began to feel unwell. He slumped onto a bench and appeared to be asleep. It was only when his young wife Josephine tried to rouse him that it became clear all was not well. Mouth-to-mouth resuscitation was attempted and an ambulance was called – but by the time they got him to hospital, Reed was pronounced dead.

Ollie Reed once claimed his ambition was to die in an Irish pub. That the pub happened to be in Malta would not have bothered him unduly. In 1989, he claimed that he would rather die than stop drinking. 'Richard Burton was hitting the bottle with Johnny Hurt the night before his death,' he once said. 'He knew it was going to kill him, but he did not stop. I don't have a drink problem. But if that was the case and doctors told me I would have to stop, I'd like to think I'd be brave enough to drink myself into the grave.'

Reed's legendary boozing exploits are testament to that. Highlights include drinking 136 pints during his two-day stag night, being sacked from the film *Cut Throat Island* after dropping his trousers and showing actress Geena Davis the tattoo on his penis, staggering onto a TV chat show and incoherently singing 'Wild Thing' while clutching a pitcher of vodka and orange, and, after a 72-hour bender the year before he died, re-enacting perhaps his most famous film scene by daring a man to a naked wrestling match in a pub in Hampstead, London. Summing up his career as 'shafting the girlies and downing the sherbie', Reed was asked by the understandably nervous insurers of *Gladiator* how much he drank. He returned the form saying, 'I only drink at parties.' The insurers wrote back, asking 'How many parties do you go to?'

> George Butterworth died, aged 36, after a late-night drinking game at Slaithwaite working men's club. During the game, he downed eight pints and eight double Pernods in 20 minutes. Afterwards the club president, David Thornton, said, "Mr Butterworth seemed to know what he was doing. He looked like he was having a good time."

The purpose of highlighting the roistering drinking career of Oliver Reed is neither to shock nor amuse. His exploits might have been extreme, but Reed was just one of a group of actors – including Burton, Hurt, Richard Harris and Peter O'Toole – gleefully dubbed 'hellraisers' by the media for their very public drinking escapades in the 1960s and 1970s. Even then,

Reed and co were merely the standard bearers of a tradition dating back as long as the acting profession itself and encompassing such luminaries as Garrick, Fields, Barrymore, Valentino, Fairbanks, Flynn, Bogart and Tracey. In the 1950s, the cult of celebrity drinking became a *raison d'être* in itself when Frank Sinatra joined forces with Dean Martin, Sammy Davis Jr and Peter Lawford to form the so-called 'Rat Pack' (Martin's act even consisted of him wandering on stage pretending to be drunk). All were heavy drinkers, and most of them ended up alcoholics. Yet all would argue that drinking – and being seen to drink – was part of their glamorous Hollywood image.

In the US, with its history of prohibition, the treatment of alcohol problems has focused almost exclusively on total abstinence.

Today, with Reed and Burton dead and Harris, O'Toole and Hurt comparatively abstemious, the mantle has been taken on by a new generation of actors happy to get hammered in public. Only recently *Gladiator* star Russell Crowe drunkenly assaulted a TV producer who had the temerity to cut a poem from his awards acceptance speech. Ollie would have been proud.

Why the acting profession should have such an affinity with the bottle was perhaps hinted at by Reed himself when he said, 'I like to give my inhibitions a bath now and then.' Hollywood psychologist Randy Kronik takes it further: 'Some actors drink themselves into their role, but you'll find most are at their most sober when they are in front of a camera. It's off-camera where the serious drinking starts. This is partly to do with the need to unburden themselves of their character, partly to do with their own insecurities within the profession, and partly because it is regarded as acceptable to do so.'

Acceptability is the word that is key to the culture of alcohol, especially when considering its high-profile consumption. It is the reason one actor can get pissed and show his penis to Geena Davis and be fondly described as an unreformed hellraiser, and why another can get busted for drugs, spend months in rehab and be called a sad loser. Abuse is abuse whatever the drug, yet the exception to the rule is alcohol. It's no secret that many of the movie greats consumed – and continue to consume – pills, coke,

Egyptian slaves working under the direction of a supervisor. The Egyptian pharaohs were partial to beer, using straws to drink ale containing wheat husks. This highly alcoholic, porridge-like substance was commonly served to slaves for sustenance. Beer was so important to the Egyptian way that full jars and beer-making ingredients were packed around the wealthy in their tombs, as provisions for the expected afterlife.

Image from the 1750s entitled 'Gin Lane', drawn by British artist William Hogath (1697–1764), illustrating the problems caused by addiction to gin. At lower centre an inebriated woman drops her baby, while a dying man sits with a cup. In the background, a dead drinker is being put into a coffin. Elsewhere, people are fighting to buy gin from a distillery, while other people give their goods to a pawnbroker in return for money to buy more drink. A man has hanged himself from a building that has become structurally unsafe because its owners are too drunk to repair it.

hash, and heroin with as much gusto as their whisky sours and martinis. But this was something they were, and still are, determined to keep behind the closed doors of their Beverly Hills mansions. But alcohol has a mystique that other drugs don't. When we think of heroin addiction we see an emaciated corpse with a syringe in its arm, yet when we think of alcohol addiction do we see Oliver Reed slumped dead in a Maltese bar? The chances are we see him heroically downing brandies while taking on the entire British navy at arm-wrestling. Perhaps we don't even think of the term 'alcohol addiction' at all. Drinkers who admire Oliver Reed do so for the same reason Sunday league footballers admire Pele and bedroom guitarists worship Eric Clapton: because here is someone who can do what you do – only inconceivably better.

WHEN WE DRINK – ALCOHOL AT WORK AND PLAY

In 1986, Norman Tebbit, the chairman and self-styled hard man of the British Conservative government, paid a visit to the headquarters of News International in Wapping, London. After being shown around the newly built, hi-tech brick fortress that was home to Rupert Murdoch's UK newspaper empire, Tebbit was shown into the office of Kelvin MacKenzie, wild-man editor of *The Sun*.

'Would you like a drink, Norman?' MacKenzie asked.

'Yes please,' Tebbit replied.

'I'm afraid we only have lemonade,' MacKenzie said sheepishly.

'You must be fucking joking!' Tebbit exclaimed.

Tebbit, of course, had every right to expect a drop of the hard stuff in the office of a national tabloid editor. After all, journalism and hard drinking have traditionally gone hand in hand from the days when almost all the UK's national newspapers were concentrated around Fleet Street. In nearby bars such as El Vinos and the Cheddar Cheese, or down in nearby Soho, it was common to see reporters congregating from opening time to closing, consuming vast quantities of alcohol, and only occasionally popping back to the office to bash out a story.

Some hacks were so bibulous that they became legends. Jeffrey Bernard spent much of his life propping up the bar of the Coach and

Horses in Soho and chronicling his drinking exploits in various magazine columns. When he occasionally became too drunk to write his column, his thoughtful editors would report 'Jeffrey Bernard is unwell' in the blank space – and the phrase became the title of a play by fellow hack Keith Waterhouse, in which Bernard was played on stage by another legendary boozer, Peter O'Toole.

One of Bernard's drinking buddies was the some-time foreign correspondent Graham Mason, a man described as 'the drunkest man in the Coach and Horses' – no mean feat. In his obituary, printed shortly after his death in April 2002, aged 59, it was noted, 'Mason was a fearsome sight at his most drunkenly irascible. Seated at the bar, his thin shanks wrapped around the legs of a high stool, he would swivel his reptilian stare round behind him to any unfortunate stranger trying to be served, and snap, "Who the fuck are you?" Sometimes this prompted a reaction, and on one occasion a powerful blow to the head sent Mason flying, with his stool, across the carpet. Painfully clawing himself upright, he set the stool in its place, reseated himself, and, twisting his head round again, growled, "Don't you *ever* do that again." '

But Murdoch's moonlight flit to Wapping, ostensibly to escape the print unions, also had the effect of changing the drinking culture of the profession. Gone were the traditional watering holes – and drinking on duty, while not outlawed, was distinctly frowned upon by the new, business-efficient management regimes. When the rest of the industry followed Murdoch's lead and fled to the steel and glass outlands of Canary Wharf in the early 1990s, Fleet Street effectively expired – and with it generations of pickled hacks to whom the pub was as important to the profession as 100-words-per-minute shorthand. 'There are plenty of wine bars in Canary Wharf,' observed one veteran reporter, 'but nowhere like there used to be. These days, you see young reporters heading for the gym at lunchtime and drinking bottles of Evian at their desks.'

The demise of traditional lunchtime drinking among journalists reflects a change of attitude towards alcohol in the UK workplace in general. While there will always be those who indulge in a liquid lunch, the tendency today is towards abstinence. In 1989, 11 per cent of working men and 6 per cent of working women admitted drinking during working hours. Ten years later, the figure was 6 per cent of men and just 2 per cent of women.

It's a trend that has been taken up in the rest of Europe too. The new generation of French and Italian businessmen, if they drink at all, now tend to stick to just one glass of wine at lunchtime; the days of big meals washed down with plenty of vino are fast fading away. Recent figures suggest that just under ten per cent of European workers in office-based jobs drink at lunchtime – a lot more than their English counterparts, but a lot less than in the past.

'Working practices have changed,' explains Paulo Chieso, a businessman from Rome. 'Ten, twenty years ago people tended to work for Italian companies and the working culture was very different. Now, in the big cities especially, everything is run by the multi-nationals, and things have changed accordingly. Now it is no longer regarded as usual to have big lunches with lots to drink, unless it is a special occasion.'

> Statistics on overall alcohol-related deaths among 15- to 29-year-olds will be presented in four main groups of countries by WHO officials. Those for Britain, EU partners, and other, more developed European states suggest one in eight male and one in 12 female deaths are drink-related. But in a group including Russia, Ukraine, Hungary, Latvia, Lithuania, and Estonia, the drink-related toll is one in three male and one in eight female deaths – across the whole of Europe, it is one in four male deaths in the age group.

For 'multi-national', read 'American', as it is there that the trend of alcohol-free workplaces first began, and where that practice is still most fervently advocated. In Los Angeles there are now dozens of restaurants and bars that exclusively serve bottles of mineral water at lunchtime, and many new employees find they must sign contracts containing non-drinking clauses. Change has been brought about because of new social attitudes towards drinking and health in general – the majority of businesses now have their own gyms or provide access to health clubs to their employees. But it is also a result of increasing concern among employers about the consequences of drinking at work. In the UK, statistics show that 25 per cent of accidents at work involve intoxicated workers. In the blue collar sector, where going for a pie and a pint at lunchtime was once a staple, spiralling insurance costs mean that turning up for the afternoon shift smelling of alcohol can mean dismissal.

ONE-OVER-THE-EIGHT, NIL – SPORT'S BOOZE CULTURE

Top sportsmen are paid millions of pounds, dollars and euros to perform – and with such vast rewards at the top level it would seem logical that they would look after themselves to prolong their careers for as long as possible. Most do: in football, the likes of David Beckham, Paul Scholes and Michael Owen are paragons of virtue who practise religiously, go to bed early and are quite rightly held up as examples to all youngsters who aspire to play for the big clubs like Manchester United and Liverpool. In doing so, they are following the lead of the army of foreign players – particularly the Italians and French – who have always combined flair with an engrained fastidiousness towards personal fitness and responsibility. Unfortunately, a large number of the dwindling band of English players good enough to play in the Premiership have continued to behave as if they are turning out for the Sunday morning pub at 11. Former internationals, such as Tony Adams and Paul Merson, have had well-chronicled drink problems. After a drink-fuelled punch up involving an Asian student, Leeds and England players Lee Bowyer and Jonathan Woodgate spent more time in Hull Crown Court than they did playing for their club. And their Leeds and England colleague Rio Ferdinand failed a breathalyzer test while at West Ham. Chelsea's Jody Morris pleaded guilty to assault causing actual bodily harm after a drinking session turned into a brawl, and was given 150 hours community service and ordered to pay £500 ($736) to his victim. His team mate John Terry was accused of braining a doorman with a wine bottle outside a nightclub. The list goes on: three England Under-21 players – Lee Hendrie, Seth Johnson and Matt Jansen – were sent home from an international tournament in disgrace after being caught drinking when there was a curfew; and England and Newcastle United starlet Keiron Dyer found himself splashed across the pages of the tabloids after taking part in a booze and sex session while on holiday.

One of the brightest stars in the British game in recent years was Paul Gascoigne, a wondrous talent on the pitch but a deeply insecure and helpless human being off it. Gascoigne emerged from the heavy drinking culture of Tyneside and, despite spells in the more sophisticated settings of London and Rome, he was unable to shake off his roots. Following his success in the 1990 World Cup, 'Gazza' became front-page news – and he didn't let the media down. Breathless accounts of his footballing prowess soon took a back seat to more lurid stories about his boozing exploits, as he was pictured trawling trendy London watering holes with a host of celebrity pals including bibulous DJ Chris Evans. During an England trip to the Far East shortly before the 1996 European Championships, he was infamously pictured tied to a dentist's chair being force-fed spirits by some of his team mates.

Of course, the culture of heavy drinking is not a new phenomenon among English footballers – although with the increased media attention now given to the game, it has become far more prominent. Gazza was high profile, but he was merely following in the footsteps of a tradition as old as the game itself. In the 1970s, George Best became better known for his boozing than for the miraculous skills, that in the 1960s, made him possibly the greatest player the game has ever seen. By the late 1990s, his skin yellow from alcohol abuse, Best was in and out of hospital for treatment for chronic liver disease and was being warned that his next drink would kill him. Before Best, there was Jimmy Greaves, a potent goalscorer who became a recovering alcoholic. And these were just the more notorious cases. For a whole generation of footballers, drinking was part of the game. Even Bobby Moore, England's World Cup-winning captain, once appeared in an advert extolling not the latest sportswear but the virtues of a few pints down the local pub.

The love of a drink, or 16, is not confined to English footballers, however. Most sports have their own cautionary tale to tell of superstars who have fallen by the wayside. Golf, a sport traditionally immersed in etiquette and professionalism, is also famed for its '19th hole' – a euphemism for the bar where players retreat after a round. John Daly, the mullet-haired American who once won the British Open and is the possessor of one of the most fearsome drives in the game, won millions of dollars on the pro-circuit only to fritter it all away on alcohol and gambling. It reached the stage where Daly was regularly walking off the course mid-round because he was unable to function without a drink. Darryl Strawberry was an equally talented baseball player with the New York Yankees – until his alcohol problems got the better of him and his career hit the rocks.

Meanwhile even the officials of Aussie Rules football, a notoriously macho sport, have been concerned about the recent binge-drinking culture affecting all levels of the game. 'Unless Australian football is able to control the use of alcohol and the way it's portrayed, then the long-term viability of the sport will be placed in question,' said Geoff Munro, from the Centre for Youth Drug Studies at the Australian Drug Foundation. 'I don't think there's any doubt that alcohol poses a bigger problem to AFL footballers than illicit drugs.'

Recent ADF research showed binge drinking was ingrained in football, revealing that a quarter of local football players and members consumed seven or more alcoholic drinks when they attended their club and 42 per cent had five or more.

One sport indelibly associated with drinking is rugby union. In clubhouses across the world, pints are sunk in heroic numbers, while drinking games such as downing a yard of ale are regular attractions – and that is just among the players. Rugby legend tells of former England player Colin Smart who was hospitalized after drinking aftershave, and a gang of England and Scotland players who played football with the priceless Calcutta Cup trophy down Edinburgh's Princes Street. International weekends in Dublin, Edinburgh and, latterly, Rome, provide much anticipated drinking bonanzas for the thousands of spectators who follow the sport. Yet, ironically, rugby is one sport where the culture of drinking remains mainly in the bar. There are virtually no famous alcoholic ex-players, and big games remain proudly violence-free on the terraces. 'Getting pissed is part of the game,' says Scottish fan Ian Munro, 'but we leave the scrapping to the guys on the pitch. That's why it's the best game in the world.'

A SOPHISTICATED TIPPLE – THE RISE OF WINE CULTURE

In July 2001, five investment bankers from Barclays Capital celebrated clinching a lucrative deal by dining at one of London's most exclusive restaurants. During the meal they downed a £1,400 ($2,061) bottle of 1982 Montrachet, an £11,600 ($17,077) bottle of 1945 Petrus, a 1946 Petrus costing £9,400 ($13,839), a 1947 Petrus at £12,300 ($18,108) and a bottle of 1900 Château d'Yquem costing £9,200 ($13,544). By the time they staggered out into the night several hours later, they had racked up a bill of over £40,000 ($59,000) on fine wine alone.

To them, it was no problem. Each had received enormous bonuses on top of six-figure salaries, and the small matter of eight or nine grand a head for the bill was peanuts. Along with their Porsches and their expensive houses, the fact that they could afford to quaff some of the most expensive wines in the world merely added to their kudos. Wine was just yet another statement of their wealth, power and influence.

It has always been the case that alcohol is freely available to anyone over the legal age who has money to buy it. But while wine has always flowed like water in the producing countries of southern Europe, in post-war Britain it was the preserve of those who could afford to import it. As a consequence, it has been a visible status symbol: wine drinkers at the top of the tree, beer and spirits drinkers halfway up and those who devoured cheap quarts of moonshine in brown paper bags down at the bottom. In the 1970s, notes Jancis Robinson, 'there were sizeable tracts of Britain in which the word wine had to be pronounced with audible quotation marks.'

> Death rates from alcohol-related liver disease rose by nearly half in a decade in the United Kingdom, according to World Health Organization advisers worried by the binge-drinking epidemic in parts of Europe.

Not any more. In the last 20 years, wine has evolved into the tipple of choice of an amorphous category of drinkers from all social classes. Along the way, it has lost its elitist mystique to the extent that it comes in cans, cartons and cardboard boxes. It is now possible to buy a perfectly acceptable bottle of wine for little more than a fiver ($7.30) from the local supermarket. Where once the selection was limited to screw-top Liebfraumilch and litre bottles of French plonk, shelves now groan with first-class produce from the New World and South America as well as respected labels from France and Italy. Today, even wine that was once prohibitively expensive can now be purchased for under £10 ($14.72). In 1986 Britons drank more than five times as much light table wine as in 1970. In 2001, it was 20 times – the equivalent of 60 bottles per head per year.

The rise in British wine consumption mirrors an increase in consumption and production worldwide after a slump that took root in the early 1980s. Figures released in 1996 showed that the leading wine-producing countries, Italy, France, Spain and Portugal, all saw production increases. The last 20 years have also seen an increase in the output of New World producers, especially Australia, America, Chile

Experts do now tend to agree that there is a positive effect from alcohol on the cardiovascular system, but only when taken in small doses and only for certain people.

and Argentina. The top four wine-consuming nations, France, Italy, USA and Germany, consume about half of the world's wine, with the French and the Italians still streets ahead in terms of production, consumption and – most would argue – appreciation. French writer Grimod de la Reyniere recalls a meeting between one French wine expert and the Prince of Wales. 'The expert told the Prince, "At a great wine we look at its play in the glass, breathe in its fragrance, and then..."

'"We drink it!" – the Prince interrupted.

"Oh, no, your Highness," the gourmand went on. "First we talk about it."'

Whether the rest of the world will ever catch up with the sophistication and expertise of the French and the Italians is debatable; they have, after all, had thousands of years' experience. Some countries, notably the Scandinavian and eastern European nations, have never shown much interest and are unlikely to bother. But there is hope that things could change. Even the British, who once regarded wine as a four-letter word, have had their tastebuds and drinking habits revolutionized by the concept of partaking of wine in pubs. Once smoke-filled drinking dens filled with

French engraving from the 1770s of two alcoholics. One has drunk too much and is vomiting into a bowl as his companion holds onto his wig to stop if from falling into the bowl as well. Underlying this caricature of alcoholism is the seriousness of this disease.

French engraving from the 1770s of three alcoholic women enjoying a drink.

1855 illustration entitled 'Very Full' depicting an alcoholic having to be supported by his wife and son. The man appears untidy while the boy is wearing no shoes, suggesting that his father spent all of his money on alcohol.

men in flat caps, market forces and social changes brought about by increased travel, prosperity and Europeanization have resulted in pubs that now serve decent food, cater for families and serve good wine. Gone is the vinegarish red and the sickly sweet white. Inconceivable 20 years ago, today even the most spit-and-sawdust bar will have a blackboard indicating a fulsome selection of Merlot, Cabernet Sauvignon and Chablis on offer.

'When I first started in the business,' says veteran Newcastle-upon-Tyne publican Peter Devenish, 'we used to have a bottle of Blue Nun behind the bar in case some bloke brought his wife in. The idea of people drinking wine in pubs was virtually unheard of. Wine was something the toffs drank. But everything has changed. These days landlords take as much pride in their wine selection as they do with their beer.'

With such enlightenment, it is tempting to believe that, as far as wine is concerned, social and cultural elitism are indeed things of the past – or at least the preserve of insufferable, stereotypical snobs like TV's Frasier Crane and his brother, Niles, whose constant bickering is often focused on who will become Grand Corkmaster of Seattle's premier wine appreciation society.

Wine-club membership is indeed booming today, people's palates are becoming more sophisticated and, thanks to the Internet, it has never been easier to order top-class wines at affordable prices.

Even the flaunting of wine as a status symbol appears to be frowned upon these days. The five Barclays Capital bankers who spent over £40,000 ($59,000) on wine in July 2001 were sacked a few months later. Their actions, it was said, were viewed as inappropriate at a time when the City was trying to present a more sober face following the end of the technology and telecoms share boom.

There will always be exceptions of course: the most expensive bottle of wine was sold at an auction at Christies of London, in December 1985. The buyer paid £105,000 ($155,000) for a bottle of 1787 Château Lafitte Claret that was engraved with the initials of Thomas Jefferson. Tellingly, perhaps, eleven months after the sale, the cork dried out, slipped into the bottle and turned the wine into vinegar.

THE YOUNG ONES – STUDENT DRINKERS

Students have always been notorious consumers of alcohol, taking full advantage of subsidized student union bars, grant cheques and the fact that they are no longer living at home with their parents. But, of late, it seems the student fraternity is having increasing difficulty handling its drink.

In the year 2000 alone, a startling number of students at UK universities literally drank themselves into oblivion. One 21-year-old Oxford undergraduate plunged 60m from a crane while twice the legal drink-drive limit; a Welsh student fell into Cardiff bay; another Oxford student fell from a window ledge to his death after a day spent drinking and a student at Stirling University choked on his own vomit outside a campus bar.

At Cambridge, the hallowed halls echoed with scandal after the Dean of St Catherine's College wrote to all students, imposing strict rules to control drinking. In the first three weeks of term, he had dealt with two cases of alcohol poisoning requiring hospital treatment, excessive drinking games at formal dinners that resulted in several women students being carried from their seats and unacceptable amounts of vomiting in the common rooms. One particular group under scrutiny was the St Catherine's Alley Catz, an all-female drinking society whose *pièce de résistance* at the end of a night on the tiles was to don cat ears and run naked around the quad.

Student bingeing is increasingly widespread, according to university medical staff, who have noted growing numbers of undergraduates admitted to casualty after heavy drinking. 'One student died purely from an overdose of alcohol,' recalls Dr Michael Sansbury of the University of Wales in Swansea. 'He did not inhale his own vomit; he simply consumed vast amounts of alcohol on his birthday and died. My impression is that the rise in drinking tallies with happy hours and vodka promotions. Bars compete to attract students. It's part of laddish British culture, something to boast about - and we've found that women drink just as much as men.'

British-based organization Alcohol Concern claim 20 per cent of men and 7 per cent of women of student age are now classed as 'mildly dependent' on alcohol, meaning that their lives are increasingly affected by daily drinking levels and hangovers.

Keeley Miles, a 21-year-old student at Leeds University – one of the largest universities in the country and at one time boasting the busiest student bar – says that, by the end of her second year, more than half her student loan had gone on booze. 'We were drinking every night, starting off in the union bar and then hoovering up cheap shots and alcopops at bars in the city. I'd get so pissed I could barely walk, and the next morning, if there was a nine o'clock lecture, you could forget about it.'

The National Union of Students (NUS), while receiving a substantial amount of its funding from its student union bars, is anxious to be seen to be doing something. Every year, it runs an alcohol awareness campaign, warning of the dangers of excessive drinking with slogans like, 'If you drink – don't do drunk'. Unfortunately, the reaction of booze-hungry undergraduates is not what they would hope. 'Yeah, they come round with their flyers,' said one 18-year-old English student, 'but we just use 'em as beer mats.'

In the USA, Michigan State University (MSU) had always enjoyed a reputation as being a party school, with a particular emphasis on hard drinking and distilled spirits. Then, back in 1999, undergrad Bradley McCue drank himself to death in a frenzied alcohol binge and MSU students became unique in the world of higher education by imposing their very own alcohol ban.

The death of McCue and an alcohol-induced campus riot a few months later persuaded students to get together with community and business leaders to create a team called ACTION, aimed at stamping out binge drinking in the faculty. 'The 10 per cent of students we have found are drinking about 70 per cent of the alcohol,' reported ACTION executive director Jinny Haas. The ACTION group also produced 33 recommendations to increase student awareness, including supporting students who choose not to drink, providing harm reduction programmes for students who drink heavily and curbing happy hours and other promotions for cheap booze.

Where once the bars of East Lansing, site of MSU campus, rocked late into the night with frat boys and sorority girls tanking down the liquor, they soon echoed to the sound of polite conversation and clinking coffee cups instead. 'Our overall living conditions improved,' said student Ben Glime. 'It was a quieter place to live. Our overall academic grad point average went up.'

The MSU initiative followed hot on the heels of research revealing that, like their British counterparts, students in the USA were drinking increasingly heavily. A study of 14,000 students in 100 American colleges found binge drinking had increased in the 1990s from 20 to 23 per cent. Students living in halls were the heaviest drinkers – 86 per cent of men and 80 per cent of women reported binge drinking.

There have been many suggestions about how to curb the problem. A report, published in the *Journal Of American College Health*, proposed that college officials should change the way that alcohol is sold and advertised around campus, and check up on prospective students' drinking histories. The report also recommended college-sponsored recreational and weekend activities to replace partying – and a halt to classes ending early on Fridays.

The facts would suggest that such initiatives – while surely admirable – are equally bound to fail. Every year, American college students drink around four billion cans' worth of beer alone, which accounts for about ten per cent of the total beer company sales in the country. That translates to some $1.37 billion (£931 million) in sales for brewing giant Anheuser-Busch and $429.7 million (£292.1 million) for the Miller Brewing Company. Hardly surprising, then, that the major brewers are keen to keep a high-profile marketing presence within the campuses. A conservative estimate places annual alcoholic-beverage producer expenditure for college marketing between $15 million and $20 million (£10.2 million and £13.6 million). The anti-drinking lobby can try their best to clamp down, but with that kind of investment at stake, there is little chance the brewers will let them.

MUSCLING IN – WOMEN DRINKERS

Figures published by Alcohol Concern (AC) in 1999 struck a severe blow to the easily dented pride of male boozers.

Women, it seems, are muscling in on their action.

The group with the fastest-growing levels of alcohol consumption, according to the AC figures, were young women. While the number of men drinking more than the prescribed government safety units remained stable at 25 per cent, the number of women over-indulging had risen from 9 per cent in 1984 to 16 per cent at the turn of the century.

Women drinking is no modern phenomenon, of course. More than 200 years ago, gin was dubbed 'mother's ruin' because of its popularity among working-class mums. And the increase in alcohol consumption levels among women today has as much to with their social and cultural surroundings as it did in the 18th century.

After just one night of over-indulgence, your body will be dehydrated (alcohol is a diuretic) and your liver will be inflamed, causing enzymes to leak into your bloodstream. You will get a headache because of alcohol waste products in your blood and your gut will be inflamed which can lead to heartburn and indigestion. Your short-term memory may also be impaired.

'It's all part of the liberating process for women,' says 30-something girl-about-town Stevie Nicholls. 'Women are smoking, drinking and screwing around. It's also a function of women starting to work like men. If you get home and you've has a crap day, you crack open a beer. Or a pack of beer if it's been really awful.'

Not surprisingly, pub chains have been quick to exploit the rise of the all-new, all-drinking ladette. The putative wine bars of the mid-1980s have developed into light, airy establishments serving healthy food and deliberately setting out to snare young, well paid females.

'Simple things like putting newspapers into the bars helps,' said Bob Cartwright, of Bass Leisure Retail, the company behind the phenomenally successful All Bar One chain. 'Women were telling us that if they are meeting someone and they are waiting on their own, it helps to be able to read. If they look round, it has been known that they will catch the eye of a predatory male.'

It's a similar story elsewhere. In Singapore, for example, the traditionally male pastime of beer drinking has been taken on with a vengeance by women – and by advertisers quick to spot a rapidly growing market. 'Women are starting to appreciate beer since it's cheaper than liqueur or wine,' says Michelle Wong, general manager of Singapore's Provignage bar. 'Half of our customers are working women, and more are trying beer.' Meanwhile, Keen Jappar, manager of the China Jump Bar and Grill, says, 'There are beer advertisements on TV and in magazines targeted at women. Their message is that beer is sophisticated.'

In Australia, a survey recently carried out revealed that 31 per cent of women aged between 23 and 28 binge drink, with the number rising to 70 per cent for 18- to 23-year-olds. Professor Charlotte de Crespigny, of Flinders University in Adelaide, says there has been an explosion in the number of young women going to bars and pubs in the past ten years. 'There has been a matching, if not a surpassing, of their male peers,' she says.

New Zealand Alcohol Advisory Council chief executive Dr Mike MacAvoy says the gradual emergence of young women drinkers is a factor in the continued rise of binge drinking in that country. 'Young women are rapidly converging on young men in the drinking pattern stakes,' he said. 'We now basically have double the population of people drinking in this fashion and double the problems arising.'

In the US, it is estimated that 66 per cent of all women drink, and there is an alcohol-related death rate of 5 per 100,000 population. This is about the same as the average European figure – although in certain eastern European countries the figure is as large as 17 (in Slovenia) and a whopping 33 in Hungary.

Mind you, novelist Laura Hird argues that women drink more these days mainly because it's bloody good fun: 'Stress and increased spending power are seen as major factors – but this overlooks the fact that we also drink because it is utterly enjoyable, a wonderful way to unwind and counteract shyness. It's a fast escape, a short holiday. Women's lives are so consumed by juggling work and family that they need quick thrills to squeeze into limited free time. Alcohol fits the bill perfectly.'

The medical evidence would appear to back this up. While excessive drinking can be deleterious for the male – shrinking the penis, denting the libido and lowering sperm count – it has the opposite effect on women. A couple of drinks boosts the testosterone levels in women's bloodstream, which perks up their libido – especially in women who are on the pill or who are ovulating.

Of course, testosterone can deepen a woman's voice and make her hairier. The ultimate irony for the woman who drinks like a man is that she could one day end up looking like one...

FOR THE KIDS – ALCOPOPS AND THE TEEN DRINKING EPIDEMIC

'I like getting pissed. You feel like you can do what you want, and you don't think about shit things like going to school the next day.'

The words of Carl, aged 12, from Liverpool. Carl, who is from a good home in a nice area of the city, had just been suspended from his school for turning up to a lesson blind drunk. He later claimed to have consumed four bottles of Hooch, a lemon-tasting drink containing a shot of vodka.

He is not alone. In a survey produced in 1997, the Welsh Youth Health Survey revealed that children as young as 11 were getting into the habit of drinking alcohol, with 1 in 10 claiming to drink at least once a week. And the consumption is rising. In 1990 the average amount of alcohol consumed by 11- to 15-year-olds was 0.8 units a week, according to the Office of National Statistics. By 1998, it was 1.6 units. At the same time, hospitals throughout the UK claimed that they were having to deal with rising numbers of youngsters suffering from alcohol poisoning. About 1,000 children aged under 15 are admitted to hospital every year with alcohol poisoning. One hospital in Liverpool revealed that in 1996 it admitted 200 youngsters with alcohol overdoses – a ten-fold increase since the 1980s. Amid the predictable furore, the finger of blame was pointed firmly at one culprit: alcopops.

Sweet-tasting, colourful and also highly alcoholic, alcopops have succeeded spectacularly in bridging the lucrative drinking gap between teenagers and their parents – so much so that it is estimated that 55 per cent of boys and 71 per cent of girls aged 16–24 consume alcopops every year.

But campaigners also point out that alcopops are also providing a palatable introduction to alcohol for young children weaned on fizzy drinks – and the same marketing ploys are to blame.

The success of alcopops is largely down to clever and aggressive marketing by the manufacturers, and by intensive research into their target audience. A study into alcopop marketing campaigns by Strathclyde University found that one major reason for their take-up in the UK is that British consumers – especially young ones – appear more willing to experiment than their counterparts in other countries.

This trend was first identified in the late 1980s, when strong ciders and fortified wines with exciting names and brash packaging came onto the market. These evolved into alcopops, and by 1998 Britain's market in these flavoured alcoholic drinks was estimated at £750 million ($1.1 billion).

Such a percentage is difficult to ignore, which is why, despite complaints from parents and statistics that showed increasing numbers of juvenile drinkers, the manufacturers became more ruthless in their targeting. One product examined was MD 20/20, otherwise known as Mad Dog, a fortified wine with an alcohol concentration of 13.1 per cent. The drink, which comes in a variety of fruit flavours, is imported from the US. It comes in clear bottles that show off their bright contents, and they also have a screw top and so are easy to carry around.

The Strathclyde researchers concluded that Mad Dog 'meets the needs and taste preferences of experimental drinkers' while the high alcohol content 'satisfies the need for rapid intoxication'. Ominously, the team concluded that manufacturers 'no longer think of themselves as in the alcohol business but in the mood-altering business.'

'Manufacturers should be aware that their products are widely consumed by under-16s and they should change their marketing strategies to reduce the appeal of the drinks to children,' said Virginia Blakey of Health Promotion Wales. 'It is important that their parents and other adults appreciate that alcopops, because they are more palatable to children than conventional alcoholic drinks, can help to establish behaviour likely to be very damaging to the health of children.'

This view of alcopops as a 'gateway' drink to the hard stuff is backed up by a survey of 8,000 young people conducted by the Schools Health Education Unit (SHEU) at Exeter University. They found that youngsters who drink alcopops consume around 50 per cent more units of alcohol per week than those who don't.

The British Medical Association points out that the problem is not so much alcopops themselves, but the way in which they are sold. The BMA's Dr Bill O'Neill said, 'The real problem is about underage sales and the promotion of alcohol among young people. There ought to be advice on sensible drinking and the context in which children are allowed to drink.'

The marketing of alcopops and other alcoholic drinks aimed at young people flies in the face of the World Health Organization's European Charter on Alcohol, signed by all member states of the EU including the UK, which says, 'All children and adolescents have the right to grow up in an environment protected from the negative consequences of alcohol consumption and, to the extent possible, from the promotion of alcoholic beverages.' The Charter suggests that each member state 'implement strict controls, recognising existing limitations or bans in some countries, on direct and indirect advertising of alcoholic beverages

> In the USA, in 44 per cent of violent incidents, victims describe their assailant as 'drunk'. Alcohol is associated with up to 70 per cent of homicides, stabbings, and beatings and 50 per cent of fights or assaults in the home.

and ensure that no form of advertising is specifically addressed to young people, for instance, through the linking of alcohol to sports'.

In the USA, where most states have a legal drinking age of 21, getting hold of illicit alcohol is regarded as a challenge by most teenagers – including those who should know better. In 2001, Jenna and Barbara Bush, the 19-year-old daughters of President George W Bush, were caught attempting to buy liquor using forged ID cards and prosecuted by a court in Texas. Amusingly, the court heard that the Bush girls' security guards were waiting outside while the attempted transaction took place.

By using the Internet, a minor can easily search for any of dozens of websites that can produce phoney ID cards and driving licences to order. 'My estimates are that approximately 20 to 35 per cent of all our youth have false identification in their possession,' said a spokesman for Maryland police. 'And some of these fake IDs are so good that we can't even detect them using these false identification manuals produced for that very purpose.'

The evidence would seem to be irrefutable that the more adults try to stop teenagers drinking, the more teenagers want to drink. It is easy to understand why if you consider the saturation levels of alcohol advertising on US television. In 1996, the Center on Alcohol Advertising revealed that more children aged 9–11 could recall the slogan of the Budweiser frogs than they could Smokey the Bear or Tony the Tiger. Meanwhile in 1994 the *American Journal Of Public Health* noted that, 'children who reported greater awareness of television beer advertising had more favourable beliefs about drinking, greater knowledge of beer brands and slogans, and increased intention to drink as adults'.

Health warnings fall on deaf ears – and, in some cases, understandably so. 'Adolescents who reported misusing alcohol were likely to engage in early sexual activity, multiple partners and unprotected intercourse 6.1 to 23.0 times more than young people who did not misuse alcohol,' claimed one US health report. 'Awesome!' was the reaction of a 15-year-old boy interviewed later by the *Washington Post*. 'Gimme a Bud!'

In fact, American health chiefs are just as concerned about the rise of alcopop culture among youngsters as the rest of the world. Dubbed 'Starter Suds' by the US media, alcopops have been tried by an estimated 40 per cent of kids aged 14–18, while twice as many 14–16-year-olds prefer them to beer. The drinks, available in lemon, apple, berry and orange flavours, showed sales of about $90 million (£61.2 million), or 4.1 million cases, in 2001.

There are alcohol advertising guidelines already in existence. In the US, alcohol advertising is extensively regulated by the Federal Trade Commission, the Bureau of Alcohol, Tobacco and Firearms and numerous state and local authorities. The main guidelines are that alcohol ads should not be directed at juveniles, and that they should not show alcohol as a substance that enhances personality or improves life. Distillers have, since the 1940s, had their own voluntary code of good practice to 'ensure responsible, tasteful and dignified advertising and marketing of distilled spirits to adult consumers who choose to drink, and to avoid targeting advertising and marketing of distilled spirits to individuals below the purchase age.'

In Europe, advertising restrictions vary – but most countries allow alcohol to be promoted as long as it does not overtly encourage youngsters to drink. The most common way of doing this is to restrict alcohol commercials until after 9pm.

Members of the Women's Christian Temperance Union (1909), who marched on Washington, DC, to present a petition supporting Prohibition

Prohibition protesters, 1923, parade in a car emblazoned with signs and flags calling for the repeal of the 18th Amendment.

Perhaps understandably, the alcohol and advertising industries argue that as alcohol is a legal product it should be legally possible for it to be advertised, and that bans on alcohol advertising would have adverse effects on the alcohol market and on the media. They also argue that there is no evidence of a link between advertising and the overall level of alcohol consumption or the amount of alcohol-related harm.

However a recent study of the impact of alcohol advertising on teenagers in Ireland found:

- alcohol advertisements were identified as their favourites by the majority of those surveyed;
- most of the teenagers believed that the majority of alcohol advertisements were targeted at young people, because they depicted scenes of dancing, clubbing, lively music and wild activities identified with young people;
- the teenagers interpreted alcohol advertisements as suggesting, contrary to the code governing alcohol advertising, that alcohol is a gateway to social and sexual success and as having mood-altering and therapeutic properties.

The rise of alcopops has coincided with the increasing number of brightly lit city centre theme bars that deliberately set out to attract younger drinkers with special offers, happy hours and racks of cheap, glossily marketed drinks. Despite the presence of doormen, under-age drinkers are confident of getting served.

The British government has acted quickly to curb what is perceived in some quarters as an epidemic of underage drinking. It is now an offence for an adult to buy alcohol for a juvenile. There are also tougher restrictions on cornershop off-licences, which means they will lose their licences if they are found to be selling alcohol to young people.

But the government has drawn the line at banning alcopops completely and Bass, which produces two-thirds of all alcopops, rejects claims that it is targeting youngsters, saying, rather, that opponents are demonizing a product that is enjoyed by 'the vast majority' of consumers.

Of course it is as hard to keep kids from drinking booze as it is to stop them trying cigarettes, drugs and sex. Alcopops might be in the firing line, but the figures show that young people are not choosy about what they drink.

02

WORLD

> 'If the pubs don't close at 11, there's no-one fighting on the way to the club between 11 and 12. And if there's no-one fighting, there's no-one in casualty. And if there's no-one in casualty, nurses will lose their jobs. And before you know it we'll have nurses begging on the streets. And all because people wanted a late-night drink!' – Al Murray

WHAT'S YOUR PROBLEM?: DRINKING EUROPEAN STYLE

When 84-year-old Juan Constantin goes for a drink, he frequents the establishment owned by his old friend Miguel. Tucked away in an anonymous backstreet of San Antonio on the Mediterranean island of Ibiza, it consists of a few rickety tables and chairs beneath a sun-faded awning. Juan likes to sit with his pals, playing chess or backgammon while sipping on a glass or two of Rioja. Sometimes Miguel will bring out a plate of *pulpo* or a bowl of olives. Occasionally, very occasionally, he will switch on the tiny portable television at the back of the bar so that the regulars can watch the Spanish football team in action. 'Miguel's place is nothing special,' Juan admits, 'but it is *civilized*.'

Juan's comments are a pointed barb at the English tourists who have turned Ibiza into the party capital of Europe, and who have imported their own brand of lager-loutishness to this picturesque island. And his drinking habits, while old-fashioned compared to the buzzing bars of the major cities on the European mainland, conform to the image of continental-style drinking being far removed from the traditionally frenzied consumption of the British.

Southern European countries traditionally tend to have the most relaxed attitude to alcohol in the world. Indeed wine, alongside olive oil and fresh vegetables, is perceived as a key ingredient in the much-touted 'Mediterranean diet' that so obsesses women's magazines in the UK. In France, Italy, Greece and Spain, the British paranoia about the effect of alcohol on the body and on the very fabric of society is regarded with a quizzical shrug of the shoulders. Alcohol is an integral part of society in the Mediterranean, largely because of the vast amounts of the stuff that have been produced in the area since the year dot, and also because it is not regarded as a big thing. Jancis Robinson notes, 'So enmeshed in Mediterranean society is the ingesting of alcohol in various forms, so 'natural' does it seem, that Alcoholics Anonymous is still viewed by many as a concept almost as ludicrous as, say, a support group called "Breathers Anonymous".'

The attitude to drinking in the Mediterranean is reflected in the availability of drink, compared to the UK and elsewhere. The concept of 'opening' and 'closing' time is alien; the very idea of being chased out of a pub with the refrain, 'Ain't you buggers got homes to go to!' ringing in their ears would, to a Greek or a Spaniard, seem the height of barbarity. Bars open when it suits them and close when the last person leaves. You can sit and drink alcohol as long as you want, but most people don't because the bar is much more than just a booze outlet. Alcohol is sold as an adjunct to the food they serve. Indeed in most bars the tourists can be easily identified as the only ones drinking without food. Ice cream, coffee and ham-and-cheese toasties sell in much bigger quantities than alcohol during the day. But if you want a drink, you can have one. In Italy, for example, it is easier to buy a drink than to find a specially licensed *tabacchi* selling cigarettes, while a bottle of mineral water is often more expensive than a bottle of house red.

It is a style and attitude towards drinking that is engendered at a young age. 'I probably first sipped wine – heavily watered down – when I was nine years old. I have grown up respecting alcohol because my parents never hid it away as some kind of evil that you can't touch until you're 18,' says Donaldo Shelliano from Rome.

It's a similar view to that of Parisian teenager Jean-Marie Laval: 'I enjoy to drink, because my family have always enjoyed to drink. We do not drink to get drunk, but in order to socialize more. Drink loosens the tongue, relaxes the inhibitions.'

And among some young Europeans, there is even genuine anger that the 'traditional' respect for alcohol is being eroded. 'All this crap about the Italians and the French being sophisticates of drink is just that: crap!' says 21-year-old Giovanni Roccante. 'You get a group of French and Italian young men together in the same bar drinking American beer, you'll get the same result as anywhere in the world – violence. It never used to be this way. American beer is the death of civilized society.'

That said, however, it would be entirely wrong to assume that all of Europe is a drinking utopia compared to the boorish Britain. The inhabitants of Norway, Finland, Iceland, Sweden and Denmark may not drink as much statistically as the French, Spanish, Italians and Greeks, but their bingeing is second to none.

To some observers, it's all to do with geography. The short days and long, cold nights in the North are as conducive to the frenzied swilling of vodka as balmy Mediterranean days are to the social sipping of wine. When the Icelandic government issued an edict proclaiming every Thursday was to be a television-free day, local police found themselves swamped by drunks desperate to find oblivion through the bottle.

To others, the 'problem' is a direct result of what they drink – which in itself is an accident of geography. Grape vines prefer warm, loamy soil to iron-hard tundra, which is why the traditional Nordic beverages tend to be rocket-fuel distillates such as akvavit, schnapps and vodka, as well as the strong lager beer perfected by the Danish brewers. Whatever the tipple, it is consumed in short, sharp doses that, Jancis Robinson observes, 'are often taken without any supporting framework of connoisseurship or even appreciation of flavour, but rather as drugs, straightforward doses of which are necessary on the route to a different state of mind.' The consequences of such high-powered bingeing are all too apparent. In Finland, for example, there were approximately 2,500 alcohol-related deaths a year during the 1990s, many as a direct result of alcohol poisoning. Around 80 per cent of victims were men, and excessive alcohol consumption among young people has been a growing problem in recent years.

Some, meanwhile, claim that it is the draconian restrictions on alcohol in Nordic countries that, conversely, have led to an increase in alcohol problems. In Sweden, wine, spirits and strong beer are sold only from state-licensed Systembolaget, which are closed at weekends and which dispense alcohol in brown paper bags. Stringent laws in Finland, banning the sale of hard liquor in all but state-run 'Alko' stores, have resulted in some creative home-brewing. The Norwegians, meanwhile, were recently summoned before the European Free Trade Association because of their restrictive alcohol policy. In both these last two countries, there is just one liquor shop for every 25,000 of the population. Compare this to Denmark, where the equation is one store to every 300 people, there is no licence required to sell alcohol, beer is enthusiastically consumed and alcohol-related deaths make up but a fraction of the statistics, and it is understandable that a popular Finnish and Swedish pastime is to hop on the nearest ferry to Copenhagen for a weekend.

VODKA, POWER, AND NAIL-VARNISH REMOVER

In the former Soviet Union, drinking is almost barbaric compared to the rest of Europe. The western side of Europe cannot really comprehend how alcohol literally spells power here. We have seen how one of Lenin's first acts after the 1917 Revolution was to annex all independent vodka production to the state, realising firstly that a sure-fire way of controlling the lumpen-proletariat was to keep them subdued by drink, and secondly that control of one of the main Russian staples would give the communists significant clout when it came to hanging on to power. Interestingly, one of Vladimir Putin's first actions when assuming the reins of power was to wrest control of vodka production from the independent manufacturers back to the state.

Putin was not the first post-Glasnost leader to appreciate the importance of alcohol to political power. In 1985 one of Mikhail Gorbachev's reforms included an attempted curb on vodka drinking and, in particular, drinking it at work. His efforts were rewarded by a marked decline in official vodka consumption but a massive increase in the production of *samogon*, or moonshine, which at one stage threatened to clear Russia's shelves of sugar. Gorbachev's successor, Boris Yeltsin, took a markedly more pragmatic view of the situation. Realising that the thriving black market was costing his government millions in lost taxes, he made the first attempts to snatch back control of the alcohol business. However Yeltsin was foiled by the same vested interests that had originally shored up his wobbly administration and was forced to back down.

Not so the gimlet-eyed Putin. Within months of coming to power, the former KGB man was flexing his considerable muscle on the industry bosses. One of Russia's most powerful vodka merchants suffered a heart attack following a boardroom coup, threats to another led to him going into hiding, while a third faced criminal proceedings after his offices were raided by Putin's 'economic crime police'. Meanwhile, state officials were empowered to make key industry appointments and clamp down on manufacturers deemed not to be pulling their weight.

> In Russia over 40% of men and 17% of women suffer from alcoholism, whilst their neighbours in Poland have suffered over 1,500 fatal alcoholic poisonings annually since 1996.

At stake is a vast domestic market – the average Russian is estimated to drink upwards of 50 litres of vodka a year, and liquor taxes bring the government almost as much revenue as the oil industry – not to mention potential export profits. But, like Gorbachev, Putin is also concerned about the quite horrendous levels of deaths directly related to alcohol consumption.

In 2000, after prices on legal spirits rose because of new duties, more than 6,000 people died in just two months as a result of drinking everything from industrial cleaning fluid and nail varnish remover to low-quality vodka priced at just 30p a bottle. In the first half of 2001, the figure had reached an astonishing 17,000 deaths. Russian deputy health minister Gennady Onischenko said the figures reflected 'the growing passion for alcohol', adding that there were two million registered alcoholics in Russia – among them 56,000 children under 14. The male life expectancy, meanwhile, has slumped to 59 years – a full 14 years less than in western Europe. The epidemic at times appears comical in its predictability: every winter thousands of people freeze to death on the streets after falling down drunk, while in the summer the rivers and lakes are full of drinkers who have drowned while swimming under the influence. Monday is by general consensus the most common day to die in Russia, following a weekend bootleg vodka binge. Just such a binge in Estonia in 2001 left 44 dead and 70 in comas after drinking illicit hooch laced with poisonous methyl alcohol.

Efforts to clamp down on drunkenness generally serve to highlight its epidemic proportions. When police in Vladivostok launched a three-day anti-drink/driving operation, they arrested a whopping 333 drivers. Over the course of the year, the figure rose to more than 17,000 convictions. Even this tally didn't match the 1,000 arrests made in a four-day crackdown in the Altai territory of Siberia.

Perhaps in keeping with the chaotic state of Russian alcohol legislation, in 1975 it was decided that the best way to cure the country of its vodka addiction was to get the public hooked on beer instead. The government launched a song encouraging people to drink beer, and even declassified it as an alcoholic drink. In the face of recent vodka clampdowns, it was only a matter of time before the brewing industry decided to act. Consequently supermarket shelves are now groaning under the weight of hundreds of different types of bottled and canned beer, much of it super-strength. Across Moscow, a bottle of beer is now almost a fashion accessory among young people, and each Russian drinks an estimated 30 litres (53 pints) a year – not much compared to the rest of Europe, but a massive increase in the last ten years. Even Vladimir Putin is reported to prefer a pint to a glass of vodka.

As a result of this recent upsurge in beer drinking, in 2001 the Russian health ministry announced it intended to ban beer advertising aimed at young people, and outlaw high alcohol brands. Deputy health minister Onischenko claimed it was in danger of becoming a deadly addiction. 'We have reports that in some cities, 10 year old children are drinking beer

One of every four alcohol drinks consumed in the world is vodka or vodka-based.

on a regular basis,' he said. However Dmitri Sitnikov, of Moscow's Bravo brewery, says beer is a healthy alternative to vodka. 'Young people are choosing beer over vodka because it is trendy. Vodka is part of the Soviet era.' With the Russian beer market having grown at an average rate of 25 per cent within the last three years – making it the fastest-growing beer market in the world – Mr Onischenko's task looks thankless. It may be time for President Putin to nationalize it...

THE STATE OF THE UNION – ALCOHOL IN EUROPE
AUSTRIA

■ **Alcohol Production** – Austria produces beer, distilled spirits and wine. The country's leading brands include Stock Brandy, Spitz Brandy and Eristoff Vodka. Just three type of spirits, brandy (non-cognac), rum and liqueurs, currently account for nearly two-thirds of Austrian consumption.

■ **Alcohol consumption** – 11.1 litres of pure alcohol per head of population annually. A study carried out in 1985 found that 11.5 per cent of adults drank daily, 33 per cent drank more than 60g of pure alcohol daily and 16 per cent abstained completely from alcohol.

■ **Alcohol Dependence And Mortality** – The number of people hospitalized for alcoholic psychosis was 24.2 per 100,000 in 1993. The death rate from chronic liver disease was 25.9 per 100,000.

■ **Legal Drinking Age** – There is no minimum legal age limit for buying or drinking alcohol, but in all nine federal states the age limit for drinking spirits in public (and for visiting bars) is 18 years.

BELGIUM

■ **Alcohol Production** – Belgium produces beer, wine, and spirits. Belgium's drinks manufacturer Interbrew was the world's fourth-largest brewer in 1996. Interbrew's share of the Belgian market remains steady at 56 per cent.

■ **Alcohol Consumption** – 10.8 litres per head per year of 100 per cent alcohol. 19 per cent of adults are frequent consumers of alcohol (at least three days a week), 36 per cent are moderate consumers and 45 per cent are infrequent consumers (less than weekly or never).

■ **Alcohol Dependence And Mortality** – Deaths through chronic liver disease and cirrhosis were 11.84 per 100,000 people in 1992, the last available figure. Death rates are approximately 50 per cent higher for

The Reverend E Scarlett enjoying beer and dominoes with some of his parishioners in their local pub in Chessington, 1924.

A group of children wait outside a pub, 1925.

men than for women. Criminal offences connected with drunkenness comprised 8-14 per cent of all criminal offences.

■ **Legal Drinking Age** - There is a minimum legal age limit of 16 years for buying alcohol.

CZECH REPUBLIC

■ **Alcohol Production** - There are over 72 breweries in the Czech Republic, and 90 per cent of them have been privatized. Plzensky Prazdroj is the largest brewery in the Czech Republic, and the country's second-largest exporter. The Czech Republic also produces and exports distilled spirits and wine.

■ **Alcohol Consumption** - The Czech Republic is one of the world's highest consumers of beer. Spirits consumption fell dramatically as a result of political changes during the early 1990s, but an increase in beer consumption compensated for this. A 1993 representative sample of males aged 20-49 in Prague showed that 28 per cent averaged 50g or more of pure alcohol per day, while 8 per cent of females aged 20-49 consumed 20g or more a day.

■ **Alcohol Dependence And Mortality** - In 1994, 40 per cent of all psychiatric hospital admissions of males were due to substance-related disorders, mostly alcohol dependence. In 1993, the death rate per 100,000 people for chronic liver disease was 16.75.

■ **Legal Drinking Age** - 18 years.

DENMARK

■ **Alcohol Production** - Denmark produces beer and distilled spirits, but is primarily a wine importer. Denmark's largest brewer is Carlsberg A/S. More than 80 per cent of Carlsberg's sales are outside of Denmark.

■ **Alcohol Consumption** - The total consumption of pure alcohol in 1996 was 15.2 litres per adult. A 1990 survey revealed that 39 per cent of adults were infrequent consumers of alcohol (less than weekly or never), 44 per cent were moderate consumers and 16 per cent were frequent consumers (three or four days a week).

- **Alcohol Dependence And Mortality** – The number of people receiving treatment for alcohol dependence was 7,943 in 1993, the last available figure, while the death rate per 100,000 people for chronic liver disease rose 13.5 per cent between 1980 and 1993.
- **Legal Drinking Age** – 16.

FINLAND

- **Alcohol Production** – Finland produces, imports, and exports beer, distilled spirits, and wine. As a consequence of joining the European Union, Finland has since separated its retail and production monopolies. Oy Hartwall AB (of which Denmark's Carlsberg owns 10 per cent) and Oy Sinebrychoff AB are the country's two largest brewers.
- **Alcohol Consumption** – In 1996 the total adult *per capita* consumption was 10.3 litres of pure alcohol.
- **Alcohol Dependence And Mortality** – The rate of treatment admissions for alcoholic psychosis was 79.3 per 100,000 in 1994. The death rate for chronic liver disease was 9.9 per 100,000 in 1993.
- **Legal Drinking Age** – 18 years for buying alcoholic beverages. Consumption during working hours is not permitted, and the Wage Agreement Act states that the worker may be dismissed if consumption interferes with work.

FRANCE

- **Alcohol Production** – Groupe Danone dominates the beer market, followed by Heineken, and the top three producers sell more than two-thirds of the beer in France. In distilled spirits, the conglomerate Louis Vuitton Moët Hennessy (LVMH) dominates the world cognac trade. France's wine industry is not highly centralized. The largest producer is the family owned Castel Frères.
- **Alcohol Consumption** – 13.9 litres of 100 per cent alcohol is consumed annually – the highest rate of consumption in the world. Here, 56 per cent of adults drink once or twice a week, 30.4 per cent drink every day or three to five times per week while 7 per cent are lifetime abstainers.

- **Alcohol Dependence And Mortality** – The death rate per 100,000 people of all ages from chronic liver disease and cirrhosis fell from 33.4 (47.7 for males, 19.8 for females) in 1980 to 15.8 (22.3 for males and 9.6 for females) in 1994.
- **Legal Drinking Age** – 16.

GERMANY
- **Alcohol Production** – Germany's 1,278 breweries face growing competition as national beer consumption and income begin to decline. Importers find that it is hard to obtain a sizeable share of the German market because access is limited, profit margins are small and Reinheitsgebot (purity laws that state that beer can only contain yeast, water, malt and hops) are strict. While Reinheitsgebot is no longer enforceable by law, Germans have come to expect it of their beer.
- **Alcohol Consumption** – Alcohol consumption in Germany declined by nine per cent from 1991 to 1995. The German Health Ministry states that 16.3 per cent of males and 30 per cent of females consumed no alcohol. More than 19 per cent of males and 10.8 per cent of females consumed 11–20g of pure alcohol per day, 17.8 per cent of males and 6.5 per cent of females consumed 21–40g per day and 7.4 per cent of males and 1.4 per cent of females drank more than 61g.
- **Alcohol Dependence And Mortality** – The death rate per 100,000 of the population due to chronic liver disease was 31.5 in 1995. The number of road traffic crashes involving alcohol per 100,000 people was 41 in 1991 and 50.7 in 1992.
- **Legal Drinking Age** – 16 for buying beer and wine and 18 for buying spirits.

GREECE
- **Alcohol Production** – Traditionally, Greece has primarily been a wine-drinking country. Imported liquors, a very small portion of the spirits market before Greece joined the European Union in 1987, account for 48 per cent of the spirits market and 7 of the country's top 10 brands.
- **Alcohol Consumption** – 6.8 litres of 100 per cent alcohol *per capita*

consumed each year. There is also a staggering 97 per cent alcohol use among adult males.

- **Alcohol Dependence And Mortality** - The death rate per 100,000 people from chronic liver disease decreased from 10.6 to 8.2 between 1980 and 1993.
- **Legal Drinking Age** - 18.

HOLLAND

- **Alcohol Production** - Holland is predominantly a beer-drinking country and is home to Heineken - the number two brewer in the world and leading beer exporter.
- **Alcohol Consumption** - 8.4 litres of pure alcohol is drunk per head annually. A 1990 survey found that 20 per cent of adults were frequent consumers (drank alcohol at least three to four days per week), 34 per cent were moderate consumers (drinking at least weekly) and 46 per cent drank infrequently (less than weekly or never).
- **Alcohol Dependence And Mortality** - Admission rates to general hospitals for alcoholic psychosis was 2.8 in 100,000 during 1992. The death rate from chronic liver disease was 5.1 per 100,000 people.
- **Legal Drinking Age** - 16 years for buying beer and wine and 18 years for buying spirits.

HUNGARY

- **Alcohol Production** - Hungary produces beer, distilled spirits and wine. Zwack Unicum, producer of a unique Hungarian distilled beverage, has a 54 per cent share of Hungary's legal spirits market. South African Breweries are the country's largest brewer, controlling 38 per cent of the Hungarian market. In 1996, Hungary's Borsod Brewery, owned by Belgium-based Interbrew, became the first brewery to brew an American beer, Rolling Rock.
- **Alcohol Consumption** - In 1995 the consumption of litres of pure alcohol per head was 2.5. A survey in 1986 found that over the preceding six months, 6.6 per cent of men never drank, 12.2 per cent drank occasionally, 19.8 per cent drank moderately, 18.8 per cent drank

regularly, 10.6 per cent were problem drinkers and 14.1 per cent were heavy drinkers. Of women, 21.4 per cent never drank, 35.7 per cent drank occasionally, 14.1 per cent were moderate drinkers, 3.5 per cent were regular drinkers, 1.6 per cent were problem drinkers and 0.8 per cent were heavy drinkers.

- **Alcohol Dependence And Mortality** – Death rates per 100,000 people for alcohol dependence have risen very rapidly during the 1990s, to the point where Hungary now reports the world's second highest death rate from alcohol dependence. The number of registered patients per 100,000 with alcoholic psychosis in psychiatric hospitals was 2,610 in 1994. However, the number of people fined for 'scandalous drunkenness' fell from 21,475 in 1965 to 6,971 in 1994.
- **Legal Drinking Age** – 16.

IRELAND

- **Alcohol Production** – The major brewer, Guinness, is the world's 14th largest and also dominates the spirits trade through its subsidiary, United Distillers.
- **Alcohol Consumption** – A 1990 survey of adults found that 5 per cent drank alcohol at least three to four days per week, 40 per cent were moderate consumers and 54 per cent drank less than weekly or not at all. And 11 per cent of males were classified as heavy drinkers (drinking more than 50 units of alcohol a week), while one per cent of females were classified as heavy drinkers (drinking more than 35 units a week).
- **Alcohol Dependence And Mortality** – Death rates per 100,000 population from alcohol dependence have risen in recent years for both men and women. The death rate from chronic liver disease was 3.1 per 100,000 in 1992.
- **Legal Drinking Age** – 18.

ITALY

- **Alcohol Production** – Heineken Italia's acquisition of Birra Moretti in 1996 made Heineken Italy's largest brewer with a market share of 38 per cent. Major wine producers include the Gallo Nero group.

- **Alcohol Consumption** - 9.4 litres of pure alcohol per head every year. Total *per capita* consumption in Italy has fallen in the last 25 years along with a decrease in wine consumption and a slight increase in beer drinking. Now 53 per cent of adults are frequent consumers (drink alcohol at least three or four days a week), 16 per cent are moderate (weekly) consumers and 31 per cent drink less than weekly or never at all.
- **Alcohol Dependence And Mortality** - Deaths from chronic liver disease fell from 32.9 in 1980 to 22 per 100,000 of the population in 2000.
- **Legal Drinking Age** - 16.

LUXEMBOURG
- **Alcohol Production** - Luxembourg produces beer, distilled spirits and wine. It is also a major trans-shipment point for alcoholic beverages in southern Europe.
- **Alcohol Consumption** - Alcohol *per capita* consumption has remained fairly steady since 1970 but it did rise in the early 1980s, mainly as a result of increased wine consumption. A study conducted in 1990 found that 20 per cent of adults drank alcohol at least three to four days per week, 31 per cent were moderate consumers (drinking at least weekly) and 45 per cent drank less than weekly or never.
- **Alcohol Dependence And Mortality** - The death rate per 100,000 people from chronic liver disease decreased from 28.7 to 15 between 1971 and 1995.
- **Legal Drinking Age** - 16.

NORWAY
- **Alcohol Production** - Norway's beer industry is dominated by the foods conglomerate Orkla, which controls Ringnes - the country's largest brewer.
- **Alcohol Consumption** - Total consumption of alcohol was approximately 7 litres of pure alcohol per adult in 1994. One per cent of the population aged 18 years and over drank daily or almost daily, 23 per cent drank once or twice a week, 23 per cent drank twice a month and 38 per cent drank once a month or less.

- **Alcohol Dependence And Mortality** - The death rate per 100,000 population from alcohol dependence has slowly been rising in recent years, and is now the world's sixth highest. The death rate from chronic liver disease and cirrhosis is 5.7 per 100,000 for men and 3 for women. According to police reports, alcohol is a contributing cause of every fifth divorce, involving about 2,000 children in those families every year. And 80 per cent of all crimes of violence, 60 per cent of all occurrences of rape, arson and vandalism and 40 per cent of all burglaries and thefts are committed while under the influence of alcohol.
- **Legal Drinking Age** - 18 for buying beer or wine and 20 for buying spirits.

POLAND

- **Alcohol Production** - Poland produces beer, distilled spirits and wine. Elbrewery Company Ltd, which is controlled by the Australian Brewpole Group, has the largest share of the Polish beer market.
- **Alcohol Consumption** - 6.7 litres per head of pure alcohol per year. The State Agency for Prevention of Alcohol Problems estimates that illegal production and smuggling totals between 20 and 25 per cent of the legal trade. About 64 per cent of adults are moderate drinkers, 10.4 per cent are classified as abusers while 11 per cent of adults abstain completely from alcohol.
- **Alcohol Dependence And Mortality** - Alcoholism rose from 1.1 to 4.3 per 100,000 people between 1980 and 1995. The percentage of homicides committed while intoxicated rose from 53.9 per cent to 75 per cent between 1970 and 1985. About 25 per cent of all divorces are considered to result from excessive drinking, and it is estimated that about one million children were being brought up in families with alcohol problems. The percentage of rapes committed while intoxicated rose from 53.2 per cent in 1970 to 81.9 per cent in 1985, which are the last available figures.
- **Legal Drinking Age** - There is a minimum legal age limit of 18 for buying alcohol but it is not effectively enforced.

PORTUGAL

- **Alcohol Production** – Portugal produces beer, distilled spirits and wine. It is a major exporter of wine.
- **Alcohol Consumption** – 13.1 litres of pure alcohol are consumed each year, which is the second highest figure in the world. Over 39 per cent of the adult population drinks at least three to four days a week, 24 per cent are moderate (weekly) consumers while 37 per cent drink less than weekly or never.
- **Alcohol Dependence And Mortality** – Deaths from chronic liver disease fell from 30.3 to 22.7 per 100,000 of the population between 1970 and 1995.
- **Legal Drinking Age** – 16, but the law is rarely enforced.

SPAIN

- **Alcohol Production** – Freixenet is a leading winery with market ventures in Great Britain, Germany and the US, among others. The Spanish beer market is also expected to grow about two per cent a year. A 1995 study revealed that Spain had more liquor outlets *per capita* than any other western European country.
- **Alcohol Consumption** – 11.8 litres of 100 per cent alcohol per head are consumed each year. In Spain, 32 per cent of adults drink at least three or four times a week while 44 per cent drink less than weekly or never. Drinking patterns vary throughout the country: in Cantabria, which has a population of just 500,000, a serious problem of excessive drinking was found among men between the ages of 16 and 65. Excessive drinking among women was, by comparison, very low.
- **Alcohol Dependence And Mortality** – 19 in every 100,000 people suffer from alcohol dependence syndrome. Deaths from chronic liver disease fell from 24.2 per 100,000 in 1980 to 18.7 in 1991, while the rates for alcohol-related burns, falls, drowning and poisoning rose from 42.9 to 44.4 over the same period.
- **Legal Drinking Age** – There is a minimum legal age limit of 16 in most regions, otherwise the age limit is 18.

SWEDEN
- **Alcohol Production** – The leading brewer, Pripps, is owned by the Norwegian food and drink conglomerate Orkla.
- **Alcohol Consumption** – In 1991 the total adult *per capita* consumption was approximately 8.5 litres of pure alcohol. A consumer survey in 1990 found that one per cent of adults were drinking almost every day, 23 per cent were drinking once or twice a week, 27 per cent were drinking twice a month, 36 per cent were drinking once a month or less often and 14 per cent were abstainers.
- **Alcohol Dependence And Mortality** – Hovering between 3 and 4 per 100,000, Sweden's alcohol dependence is relatively high by global standards. The death rate for alcohol-related burns, falls, drowning and poisonings has fallen – it was 44.2 in 100,000 in 1992. A 1992 study of psychiatric patients showed that 87 per cent of attempted suicides were performed after drinking and 86 per cent of all violent episodes took place when the assailant was drunk.
- **Legal Drinking Age** – 18 years for buying alcohol in restaurants, and an age limit of 20 years for buying alcohol in liquor stores.

SWITZERLAND
- **Alcohol Production** – Switzerland produces beer, distilled spirits and wine. Two large brewers produce two-thirds of the nation's beer – the number of brewers has fallen by half since 1970 to 28.
- **Alcohol Consumption** – In 1995, the estimated total adult consumption was 11.8 litres of absolute alcohol per head. According to the Swiss Institute for Prevention of Alcoholism, 32 per cent of 45–54-year-olds consume alcohol one or several times daily. The most frequent and highest consumption occurred among the Italian Swiss, followed by the French Swiss and, lastly, the German Swiss.
- **Alcohol Dependence And Mortality** – The number of alcohol-dependent people is estimated to be about 150,000. The death rate from chronic liver disease is 8.3 per 100,000 people.
- **Legal Drinking Age** – 16 years for buying fermented beverages and 18 years for buying distilled beverages.

UKRAINE
- **Alcohol Production** - Ukraine produces beer, distilled spirits and wine. The Seagram Company has formed Seagram Ukraine Ltd in an effort to produce, distribute and market new and existing spirits in the Ukraine. Illegal imports of spirits have gained in significance in Ukraine in the late 1990s.
- **Alcohol Consumption** - The latest recorded figure was 3.4 litres of pure alcohol per adult in 1993, although the unofficial figure is more like 11.2 litres.
- **Alcohol Dependence And Mortality** - The death rate per 100,000 people from chronic liver disease and cirrhosis was 16.1 (25.2 for men and 9.6 for women) in 1992.
- **Legal Drinking Age** - 21.

HAPPOSHU DAYS ARE HERE AGAIN – ALCOHOL IN THE FAR EAST

Perhaps it was because it was such a rarity that the punishment was so harsh, but when 27 people died and 200 were hospitalized after drinking bootleg spirits with a lethal methanol content, authorities in the northern Chinese province of Shanxi came down on the culprits severely. Days after the incident, which occurred in 1998, more than 33 people were being interrogated; within weeks six had been convicted and executed.

China takes its drink seriously, and has done for thousands of years. Indeed, the very process of consuming alcohol is perceived by many as an act of great symbolism. The Chinese do not understand the West's apparent disregard for drink; the way we abuse it and the way we allow it to ruin our lives. In Chinese culture, alcohol is consumed with equal relish - but only when the time is right. It appears at all major social ceremonies, such as birthday parties for old folk, wedding feasts and sacrifices, where it is a symbol of happiness and respect. It is also well regarded, in moderation, for its health-giving properties; it is not uncommon to find people soaking traditional Chinese medicine in liquor to achieve a better effect.

China's predominant alcohol produce is distilled spirit, the most famous being Maotai, a 55 per cent liquor made of wheat and sorghum that has been made for centuries in Maotai Town in the Guizhou province. But this is

Raid on a basement distillery in Mulberry Street, New York (1925), where a group of Orientals were suspected of making hooch during Prohibition.

Directions to a speakeasy written on the roadside during the Prohibition in America, c1925.

not to suggest that the Chinese have dispensed with beer. Even the most downmarket Chinese restaurant in the UK these days is not complete without imported Tsingtao beer, produced in Pingtung by the Tsingtao Brewery Group, China's biggest beer maker. Founded by German investors in 1903, Tsingtao has become famous for its bold commercial strategy. It is one of the country's best-known export brands, and it owns around 45 beer firms on the mainland. It was also the first Chinese firm to float on the Hong Kong stock exchange.

Compared to Chinese reserve, the Japanese attitude to alcohol borders on the reckless. Public drunkenness is not only tolerated on the streets of Tokyo and Osaka, it is actively encouraged and approved of. A high-powered businessman, for example, is not viewed as having won his spurs unless he is seen tottering out of a saké bar at two in the morning after an all-day session. As long as you don't make too much of a fool of yourself, it seems that anything goes. One reason for this, perhaps, is that instances of alcohol-induced violence are scarce. Another is that the health damage from alcohol abuse is largely ignored by Japanese society, despite an estimated two million people with alcohol dependency. A typical example of the

In Uruguay, intoxication is a legal excuse for having an accident while driving.

Japanese *laissez-faire* attitude towards alcohol consumption is during the annual *hanami* ceremony, which celebrates the blooming of cherry trees in spring. During *hanami* it is customary for thousands of people to cram into 'flower-viewing' areas to observe the cherry blossom and get smashed. In 2001, 55 people in Tokyo were rushed to hospital suffering from acute alcohol poisoning on one night, while an average of ten people a day required attention for excess drinking during the five day festival. 'People tend to drink too much when they're outdoors because of the relaxed atmosphere of being outside,' one official said stoically. He then advised merrymakers, 'Please don't empty a glass of alcohol in one go or force other reluctant people to do so because it can be dangerous.'

What has been making Japanese drinkers even happier recently is the advent of *happoshu*. The word means 'fizzy alcohol' and, while it looks and tastes like beer, *happoshu* is in fact made predominantly from corn starch. A can is 40 per cent cheaper than beer, but has the same alcohol content, so it has taken off like a rice paper house on fire. Introduced by the Kirin Brewery in 1994 as a method of avoiding tax on malt and barley, it currently occupies 42 per cent of the domestic market with almost 2.5 billion litres being sold in 2001. 'We love beer but the taste of *happoshu* is similar and you get much more for your money,' said one happy Japanese drinker. As yet, there are no plans to export it overseas, as it would not have the same tax advantage.

TEETOTAL COUNTRIES AND NOT-SO TEETOTAL COUNTRIES – THE REST OF THE WORLD

For the Republic of Ireland football team's much-travelled fans, it was a bit of a quandary. The final whistle had gone at the end of an unbearably tense match and, for the first time in 12 years, they had qualified for the World Cup Finals. Normally, such news would be celebrated with several days of joyous boozing. But, on this occasion, the *craic* was distinctly muted. They were, after all, in Teheran, capital of Iran and, as everyone who had made the trip soon discovered, in Iran booze is banned.

'Some of the lads back home were saying Iran was dry,' said one bemused Irish supporter, 'but I thought they just meant there was a lot of desert and stuff like that.'

Ironically, had the thirsty Irish ventured further into Teheran than the football stadium and the airport, they might have been surprised by the amount of alcohol available. For while Iran is officially teetotal, like many Islamic countries in the 21st century, the tide of alcohol is becoming increasingly difficult to repel. In the streets of Teheran, for example, youths on motorbikes act like mobile off-licences, peddling illicitly imported beer from Holland and Australia and vodka from Azerbaijan, while in the richer suburbs even supermarkets do a trade in under-the-counter booze. Of course, they risk the wrath of the religious police – but only if they are caught, and it is increasingly easy to avoid apprehension. Even in the days of the Ayatollah Khomeini, illicit booze was often supped behind closed doors.

In countries like Jordan, which have become as westernized as is possible for a Muslim country, drink is quite easy to obtain, as it is in Iraq. Dubai is awash with hotel bars and nightclubs, while for those who prefer to take their tipple in a brown paper bag there are numerous illegal off-licences selling bootleg hooch at knockdown prices.

Nowhere in the Islamic world is the conflict of alcohol dependence and religious temperance better illustrated than in Saudi Arabia. Here is a country that is so fervently opposed to the consumption of alcohol that it recently jailed and sentenced to 75 lashes a Filipino businessman who had the misfortune to attempt to enter the country carrying a box of liqueur chocolates. Yet it is also a country where 'sadeeki' – illicit homebrewed palm juice liquor – is distilled by impoverished Filipinos and peddled throughout the souks by Yemenis and Indians, and where a lucrative smuggling business has built up with

> In Nigeria (the brand's third largest market) Guinness is almost twice the strength of the pint on sale in the UK and in Ireland. This anomaly dates from the 19th century when a higher alcohol content was used as a natural preservative for the long journey out to the colony.

neighbouring Gulf states like Bahrain. And, of course, it is a country in which westerners are allowed to drink to excess within the walls of their own expat compounds – and where a number of mysterious bomb attacks have been ascribed to a vicious gangland-style war for control of the booze that flows in and out of the compounds.

The lesson would appear to be that religious teachings backed up by the threat of floggings will not deter those who want a drink. Ingenuity is the name of the game. In the teetotal United Arab Emirates municipality of Sharjah, for instance, inspectors were horrified to discover that residents were contentedly getting smashed on supposedly non-alcoholic malt beer that had been allowed to sit on shelves so long it had begun to turn alcoholic.

There has never been any danger of an alcohol ban in Australia, however. Indeed the modern continent was populated largely by the dregs of London's Gin Lane, who were kept docile by imported rum. 'Colonial Sydney was a drunken society from top to bottom,' writes historian Robert Hughes. 'Men and women drank with a desperate, addicted, quarrelsome single-mindedness.' Modern perceptions of Australia do not veer too far from the impression of the no-nonsense, beer-swilling Ocker – an impression milked to great effect by the Australian brewing industry itself, what with

Paul Hogan and his 'Amber Nectar' drop of Foster's and the rogues gallery of characters seen drinking Castlemaine XXXX. Indeed the image of the peroxided Australian popping a tinny and sticking a prawn on the barbie has become akin to a national identity. Alcohol, especially beer, is indelibly associated with social occasions and it doesn't seem to be doing them too much harm. In 1997, for example, just 2.8 per cent of all deaths on the continent were alcohol-related, and most of those were confined to remote farming areas where heavy drinking is largely par for the course.

A recent development has been the boom in Australian-produced wine. The likes of Jacob's Creek and Lindemans are now ubiquitous on the dining tables and supermarket shelves of the UK, where their unprepossessing nature and low retail price have proved to be the catalysts for the wine revolution in this country. The most surprising thing about this is that it took until the mid-1990s to happen, as Australia has always been a fervent wine-drinking nation. In fact, until 1984, domestic wine was untaxed.

Wine exportation is also thriving across the water in New Zealand, although there alcohol has had a less free-and-easy ride over the years. Perhaps reflecting the puritanical nature of its Scots settlers, the country has always had a strong temperance lobby, and total prohibition nearly became a reality in the early years of the 20th century. Until 1967, pubs were not allowed to open in the evening and in 1999, when the legal drinking age was lowered from 20 to 18, pubs and off-licences were permitted to open on Sundays and supermarkets allowed to sell beer as well as wine, it happened in the face of strong opposition from the Ministry of Health as well as public health organizations.

But, in many ways, New Zealand drinking culture is very similar to that of Australia. Only nine per cent of the population are abstainers, while alcohol consumption remains a resolutely male pastime associated with a passion for rugby. In the mid-1980s, one medical researcher who studied male drinking rituals over the course of 18 months pinpointed no less than 43 different drinking games in a single province.

The drinking culture in South Africa, on the other hand, is as grim as its recent history. Until 1962, alcohol consumption was the sole preserve of the white minority – at least officially. In reality, black workers on the

Cape wine farms were victims of the 'dop system', in which a substantial part of their wages was paid in cheap booze. The deleterious effect of this reckless policy is only now being identified, with the Western Cape having the highest instances of Foetal Alcohol Syndrome in the world and alcohol abuse recently being identified by the director of public prosecutions as one of the country's main social problems. Although there is some evidence of young South Africans learning to moderate their drinking in tune with the post-Apartheid image of the nation, the social effects of generations of abuse will take many years to eradicate.

The rest of Africa remains comparatively unsophisticated when it comes to alcohol. In countries where it is not forbidden by Islamic law, imported spirits and beer are consumed by the rich elite, while the rest of the population either abstains or makes do with cheap bootleg liquor made from sorghum, honey, sugar cane, palm sap and even tea leaves and pineapple. But even this most basic hooch has been banned by some authorities which, of course, presents inevitable problems, not to mention tragedies, of its own. In 1998, a month after legislation banning the sale of some traditional alcoholic drinks was passed in Kenya, 80 people in Nairobi died after drinking illegally brewed alcohol laced with methanol. Two years later, in one of the country's most infamous scandals, nearly 200 died after consuming the same brew, known locally as *chang'aa*. Even in the countries where Islamic law forbids alcohol, it does not stop the poor from trying to get out of their heads on home-brew. In 2001, two men found guilty of drinking alcohol were flogged before large crowds in the northern Nigerian city of Kano after they became the first people in the state to be sentenced under new Islamic laws. Both men received 80 lashes; one later promised never to drink again and said he felt happy that he had been cleansed of his sins.

ALCOHOL GUILT – DRINKING IN THE USA
In the cult US cartoon series *The Simpsons*, the numbskull father Homer spends much of his time drinking Duff beer in Mo's Tavern – although it is puzzling why anyone, even Homer, would want to drink there. The bar is a dingy, windowless shed with only a crummy sign above the door, and it is populated with booze-sodden, brain-dead losers.

But *The Simpsons* is regarded as one of America's pithily observed satires for a reason. Mo's Tavern accurately reflects a North American attitude to alcohol that is forged in guilt and which, to this day, regards drinking as something shameful that should be hidden away. Prohibition may have come to an end 70 years ago, but it *happened*, and its legacy lingers on in the American psyche; it is illegal to buy drink until you are 21 – the highest age limit in the world – and even the duty charged on beer, wine and spirits is often called the 'sin tax'. Indeed, large areas of the US remain resolutely 'dry', and the idea of getting a drink in certain parts of Utah, Kansas and Arkansas is out of the question unless you are prepared to go sneaking around private drinking clubs or distil your own liquor. In America, even the drunks hide their bottles in paper bags.

Ironically, Americans do not consume much alcohol. The far-flung reaches of the 50 states may encourage heavy drinking through their sheer remoteness, but in the most populous states of the eastern and western seaboards the average *per capita* consumption is around six litres of pure alcohol a year – a mid-table position in terms of global consumption. And that figure is going down all the time, especially in the cities where among the health-fixated, moneyed, upwardly mobile set it is almost unheard of to order wine with lunch.

Not that America has ever had much of a love affair with wine. The main wine-growing areas of California have failed to make much of an impact on the global market, largely because they have never made much of an effort – anyone who remembers the Paul Masson urine sample-style bottles of plonk from the 1970s will understand why this should be the case. Traditionally, America has divided itself into two distinct drinking camps: the blue-collar drink of choice is beer, while the elite classes drink spirits. Despite a rise in beer 'connoisseurship', thanks to the growing number of micro-breweries in cosmopolitan cities like New York and Boston, this division remains pretty much standard. Brewers such as Budweiser and Schlitz target the ordinary guy who likes to down a six-pack on his porch after a hard day's work, while the likes of Brown-Foreman caters for the lawyer who prefers to mull over that day's cases with a Jack Daniels on the rocks.

Yet the overriding sense of guilt will not go away when it comes to Americans and alcohol. 'It's like masturbation,' says New York journalist Todd Jackson. 'Everybody does it, but you just don't talk about it in public. And some people still reckon it makes you blind and drives you mad.' It is this attitude that explains why it was in America that Prohibition took such a hold, why it was in America that Alcoholics Anonymous was founded and why it is in America that there are an estimated 13,000 alcohol rehabilitation centres ready to cure those who have strayed from the path of righteousness. In the 1970s and 1980s, it was almost *de rigueur* for celebrities to be seen emerging from the Betty Ford Clinic and heading straight for the nearest chat show where they could tell the world how they had renounced the demon drink.

25 per cent of domestic violence is drink-related in Spain, whilst in Sweden 87 per cent of attempted suicides were attributed to alcohol in 1992.

In most of these centres, the focus is not upon the alcoholic but upon the effect of their drinking on his or her family. Indeed, if you are an alcoholic in the USA you are not merely letting yourself down, but everyone who is associated with you. To drink is not only irresponsible, it is positively un-American. Hence the almost religious zeal with which, in the 1970s, the anti-drinking brigade fell upon the discovery of Foetal Alcohol Syndrome,and the guilt with which a generation of mothers watched their children flunk school. Even today it shows no sign of abating. In 2001, a woman from Racine, Wisconsin was charged with attempted murder after giving birth to a child with FAS, while in 1995, a San Jose judge ordered a woman with three FAS children first to jail and treatment, then to submit to monthly pregnancy tests and to enrol in a live-in drug and alcohol programme should she become pregnant during the five years she was on probation.

Another wholly sinister development in the backlash against alcohol is the unchecked rise in lawsuits. In America, it is not unheard of for the victim of a drunken driver to sue the person who served the driver with the drink that took him over the limit. It has even been the case that the drunken driver has sued the person who allowed him to drive home drunk.

'It happens all the time these days,' says Boston-based attorney Paul Veradian. 'I've been to parties where the host insists you hand over your car keys so he can put them in his safe. I've also heard of guests having to sign waivers releasing the host of any blame should they be caught drink driving. One guy even made people blow into a breathalyzer before they went home. It's crazy!'

The main way America's alcohol fixation has manifested itself, however, is through its policy towards drink and young people. As previously mentioned, the minimum legal drinking age (MLDA) is 21, and this is a deliberate measure aimed at nipping the perceived problem in the bud. The policy first saw the light of day after Prohibition and remained that way until the early 1970s when, following the lowering of the voting age, 29 states lowered their MLDA to 18, 19 or 20. However, the powerful anti-alcohol lobby soon employed its own scientists to provide the proof that the MLDA of 21 should be restored. They duly unveiled statistics proving that, among other things, motor vehicle crashes – the leading cause of death among teenagers – increased significantly among teens when the MLDA was lowered, and that although it was not a watertight way of stopping youngsters drinking, it made them drink less and suffer fewer alcohol-related injuries and deaths. Armed with these figures, so-called 'citizen advocacy groups' pressured the states to restore the upper age limit. Such was the pressure they applied that, between September 1976 and January 1983, 16 of the original 29 upped their MLDA. Seeing resistance from other states and being concerned that teenagers would simply travel across state lines to purchase their booze, the Reagan administration unveiled the Uniform Drinking Age Act in 1984, which threatened the rebel states with a reduction in the subsidy of federal transportation costs unless they raised their age limits. The rebels caved in almost immediately.

> In France over 40 per cent of fatal traffic accidents – 4,000 deaths a year – and overall 43,000 deaths, 9 per cent of the total, were linked to drink in 1997.

Despite this, health organizations in the USA have an almost pathological fear of the effects of alcohol on its teenagers. 'Teen tipplers:

America's underage drinking epidemic!' screamed a report by the National Center on Addiction and Substance Abuse (NCASA) at Columbia University in February 2002. The report pointed out that children under the age of 21 drink a quarter of all alcohol consumed in the USA, and that more than five million high-school students admit to binge drinking at least once a month.

'By any public health standard, America has an epidemic of underage drinking that germinates in elementary and middle schools with children aged 9–13 and erupts on college campuses where 44 per cent of students binge drink and alcohol is the number one substance of abuse – implicated in date rape, sexual harassment, racial disturbances, drop-outs, overdose deaths from alcohol poisoning and suicides,' said NCASA chairman Joseph Califano, pointing out that teenagers who drink are seven times likelier to engage in sex, while alcohol has been proven to damage young minds, limiting mental and social development. 'No other substance threatens as many of the nation's children,' he added. 'Eighty per cent of high school students have tried alcohol, while 70 per cent have smoked cigarettes and 47 per cent have used marijuana. Drinking is teen America's fatal attraction. How did we get here? We have to point the finger at ourselves. Parents see drinking and occasional bingeing as a rite of passage, rather than a deadly round of Russian roulette. College administrators and alumni have played Pontius Pilate, washing their hands and looking away as students made beer, alcohol and binge drinking a central part of their college experience... The pervasive influence of the entertainment media has glamorized and sexualized alcohol and rarely shown the ill-effects of abuse... Television runs ads glorifying beer on sports programmes watched by millions of children and teens... The interest of the alcohol industry – especially those who sell beer – in underage drinking is understandable, if appalling.'

While the sentiment is obviously meant well, the language in which it is couched is argued by many to be extremist and self-defeating. 'It's like the bad old days of the Prohibitionists,' says Paul Veradian. 'Nobody wants to see teenagers smashed out of their heads, but it's scaremongering to use words like "epidemic" and "fatal attraction". The best way to get kids to do something is to tell them they can't do it, and not allowing them to drink until they are 21 just encourages them to beat the system. When the President's daughters get caught trying to buy liquor, you know the system is wrong.'

03

HISTORY

> 'Without question, the greatest invention in the history of mankind is beer. Oh, I grant you that the wheel was also a fine invention, but the wheel does not go nearly as well with pizza.' - Dave Barry

ALCOHOL: THE EARLY YEARS

It is entirely appropriate that no-one can remember by whom or even when alcohol was first discovered. There must have been one hell of a morning after, though...

The most compelling evidence points to the Middle East 10,000 years ago – although archaeologists have discovered evidence of a basic form of fermentation from some 2,000 years earlier. The first brew was most probably a wine made from date palms, and probably came about by accident when a farmer left some of his harvested fruit to rot in water. It is ironic that, as we shall discover, the part of the world that first invented alcohol now leads the way in banning it.

Initially, fermentation was a way of getting safe, clean fluids into the body – although in the spirit of alcoholic braggadocio these origins have become glamorized. According to ancient legend one Persian king, who was very fond of grapes, hid some in an earthenware pot marked 'poison'. The jar was forgotten until one of his harem, tired of life, found the jar and drank its contents. It was so delicious that she took a cup to the king who drank from it and then instructed that grapes should be allowed to ferment and be served to all his guests. In 1750 BC, King Hammurabi of Babylonia issued a royal decree forbidding anyone to tamper with beer. Penalties were severe: any brewer found guilty of watering down his ale was ordered to be executed.

Wall paintings suggest that the Egyptian Pharaohs were very partial to a drink of wine with their meal, but we know they were keen beer makers too because they invented straws for drinking ale containing wheat husks. This porridge-like substance was most commonly served to slaves for sustenance, but was also highly alcoholic. Indeed it was the Egyptians who first documented the social problems associated with drunkenness. It was also the Pharaohs who instituted the first formal beer taxes, reasoning that such was the cost of the monuments, pyramids and tombs that such taxes would fund public works and curb drunkenness. Interestingly, beer was considered so valuable it was established as one of the ways to actually pay the tax.

Beer was so important to the Egyptian way of life that even death could not separate the two. As a common part of burial customs, the wealthy arranged for meals augmented with jars of beer to be packed around them in their tomb, as provisions for the expected afterlife. Recent archaeological finds have revealed that the Egyptians were ready for any eventuality, as beer-making ingredients were also packed into tombs in case the journey took so long dead people had to start brewing their own.

Meanwhile, in South America, emerging cultures were also adopting beer into their traditions. Religious leaders prepared human sacrifices by first getting them intoxicated with beer before leading them to the altar and death. Some tribes cremated their dead and used the ashes to 'finish' the beer. Women brewers in these cultures held a position of honour, and were buried with their brew pots and tools around them.

In Jewish culture, the history of alcohol begins with Noah and the Flood. In Genesis 21, we are told that after landing on Ararat, one of the first things Noah did was to plant a vineyard, after which he 'drank of the wine and he was drunken'. The New Testament tells of Sennacherib and Nebuchadnezzar planting vast vineyards in order to grow wine, and it is true that it was not until the Israelites began producing wine that it became an art form. Their technique was to gouge deep fermenting holes out of bare rock, and channels between various holes at different heights. This enabled them to run the top layer of wine down a gully into one at a lower level, thus leaving the sediment behind.

The Greeks developed a taste for highly spiced wines, including an almost undrinkable brew made from pine resin that was a very early version of retsina. They also enjoyed adding seawater to their wine, believing it to contribute sweetness to the brew. They were sufficiently in awe of the effects of alcohol that they worshipped a god of wine, Dionysus, who is their equivalent of the Roman god Bacchus.

In ancient history, few relished their wine like the Romans. Blessed with a climate perfect for the growth of abundant vines, they drank in heroic quantities – but were also the world's first connoisseurs. In the 1st century AD, Pliny wrote what was effectively the first wine manual in the 14th volume of his *Natural Histories*, although he himself was no great fan, observing, 'There is no department of man's life on which more labour is spent. As if nature had not given us the most healthy of beverages to drink, water.'

The Romans developed a method of brewing by fermenting the fruit of the 'oine' vine and adding honey, spices, herbs and pine cones. The resultant brew became the staple drink throughout the Empire – and in the case of countries like Gaul, modern-day France, began a relationship with viticulture that exists to this day.

They were also great innovators when it came to wine making. Long before the invention of corks, the Roman's used to pour a layer of olive oil on top of their wine vats to seal them. The wine itself was aged in stone jars, and the liquor was sterilized with sulphur. Such techniques, along with so many other examples of Roman sophistication, were lost when the Empire imploded. Sterilization was frowned on, and wine was kept in poorly sealed wooden casks that allowed air to sour the brew.

Although it is thought the Chinese had been brewing their own beer from rice for hundreds of years, it was not until around AD 400 that the first European wine-making techniques arrived there. These were taken to them by merchants travelling on the Silk Road, and were eagerly adopted by the Chinese.

US customs officials examine steel torpedoes on the schooner *Rosie*, 1926. The torpedoes are filled with whisky and designed to be towed undetected through the water to beat Prohibition in the USA.

A group of the first US troops in wartime Britain enjoy a quiet beer outside a village pub.

American writer Ernest Hemingway (1899–1961). An heroic drinker, a typical day's consumption alcohol for Hemingway would begin with a breakfast of tea and gin followed by regular shots of absinthe, whisky, and vodka. Lunch would consist of three or four large martinis washed down with five or six bottles of wine. 'Papa' claimed it helped him to write. His drinking exploits certainly contributed to his image as a macho man's man. Unfortunately, they also contributed to hypertension, kidney and liver disease, œdema of the ankles, high blood urea content, mild diabetes, haemachromatosis, recurrent muscle cramps, chronic sleeplessness, and sexual impotence. He committed suicide in a fit of depression at the age of 62.

No less than six liquor stores can be seen in this Chicago street, photographed in 1950. In an area known for its derelict population, the city fathers, goaded by public indignation, would sometimes close down a number of these establishments.

Wine had also reached British shores, largely for the consumption of its Roman colonists. But one of the reasons the British Isles evolved such a predominantly beer-drinking culture is because the Angles, Saxons, Jutes and Vikings, who filled the Roman void in the subsequent years, allowed viticulture to decline so spectacularly. For them, there was little allure in drinking 'vinegar' and, besides, while the Romans had been perfecting the art of wine making, the so-called savages had been knocking up a bit of the hard stuff themselves. In their case, the preferred tipple was mead, ale and cider – and usually as much as they could get of all three down their necks at once. A favourite Anglo-Saxon party trick was downing the contents of a hollowed-out horn in one, a drinking game immortalized by the 'yard of ale' challenge seen in rugby club bars throughout the world today.

Brewing was a family concern, with each household making and drinking its own ale – which made sense in a time of minimal sanitation and virtually non-existent fresh drinking water. Some families were better at brewing than others, and would happily cash in on this by selling pitchers of their ale. Eventually, the concept of the ale-house, the forerunner of the public house we know today, began to develop, as did the idea of mass brewing. It was certainly the Saxon kings who made the first laws regulating brewing activities in Britain.

In Scotland, the Picts were renowned both for their ferocity in battle and their expertise in brewing. One of their most highly prized brews was 'Heather Ale'. Legend has it that when the Picts were finally conquered by a rival clan, the king was cornered on the edge of a cliff. Offered leniency if he divulged the secret of Heather Ale, he chose instead to fling himself into the abyss, choosing death rather than disgrace.

The Dark Ages saw the rise of Christianity, and with it the growth in power of the Church. Recognizing the galvanizing effect of beer on the masses, the clergy quickly utilized their own brewing skills to monopolize the market and thereby accrue large amounts of revenue. Taxes on beer were levied in the form of licensing fees, in particular targeting the production of Gruit, a mixture of herbs used by brewers before the advent of hops. Laws dictated by the Church limited the availability of Gruit to brewers, and only those Gruit suppliers approved by the Church could provide the brewers with the secret mixture.

The clergy were certainly lacking in forgiveness if anyone tried to cheat them out of their beer tax. In Aix-la-Chapelle, the council of 1272 confronted the non-payment of beer taxes with severe penalties. Brewers found guilty of avoiding or cheating on taxes were punished by having their right hands chopped off. The council also identified the widespread practice among tavern keepers of avoiding tax by importing beer without paying the tariff. To stop this, they ordered that any tavern avoiding the tax should be destroyed.

It did not take long for the brewing industry to take shape in Europe, and for trade in alcohol to thrive. By the reign of Henry IV at the beginning of the 15th century, the first brewers' guild – 'the Mistery of Free Brewers' – had been established. In 1437 Henry VI granted a charter to the Worshipful Company of Brewers, giving them effective control of all brewing activities within the City of London and its suburbs 'for ever'. This right still exists today.

The connections of the brewing guilds stretched far into Europe, and so it was inevitable that British merchants began to deal with their counterparts across the Channel. English ale had a good reputation abroad – 'decocted from choice, fat grain... a drink most wholesome, clear of dregs, rivalling wine in colour and surpassing it in flavour' according to one 12th century writer – while by the 14th century a thriving European wine trade was also firmly in place.

THE NEW WORLD – ALCOHOL ARRIVES IN AMERICA

They may have had a reputation as being God-fearing Puritans, but when the Pilgrim Fathers landed at Plymouth Rock in 1620 their immediate concern was not about setting up their colony but their dwindling supplies of beer. 'We could not now take time for further search or consideration; our victuals being much spent, especially our beere,' wrote one pilgrim. In fact, beer was a vital supply on the *Mayflower* and on every other ship that travelled long distances in the 17th century, as it was deemed far safer for the crew than water. One of the main reasons the Pilgrims were dumped at Plymouth Rock, further north than they expected, was because the *Mayflower*'s mercenary crew were concerned about getting back to England before their beer supplies ran out.

The Pilgrims were by no means the first arrivals in the New World; colonists from England, Holland, Spain and France had been landing on the eastern seaboard for 20 years. Some were more successful than others, and it was at the thriving Dutch colony on the tip of Manhattan Island that the continent's first private brewery was established in 1612. A decade later, the Dutch opened the first public brewery in nearby New Amsterdam, now known as New York.

Beer making was at first something of a struggle in the New World, due to the lack of suitable grain. William Penn, founder of the state of Pennsylvania, was able to open a brewery in 1638 but only because the state was one of the few that could sustain a barley crop. Elsewhere, alternatives such as corn, persimmons, maple syrup, pumpkins and spruce bark were all tried and discarded, and for many years the colonists drank cider made from the abundance of apples. Even today, the US has only three hop-growing states – Idaho, Washington and Oregon.

> Evidence from countries that ban spirit advertising suggests they had 16 per cent lower alcohol consumption than countries with no bans; and those with bans on beer and wine advertising had 11 per cent lower alcohol consumption than those with bans only on spirit advertising.

Once grain and hops supplies began arriving in earnest from England, ale and beer became a major dietary staple in the colonies. Everyone drank it, even babies; it was not uncommon for drinking to begin before breakfast, and it continued with every meal throughout the day. It was both nourishment and refreshment, and 'ale breaks' were as ubiquitous and numerous as 'tea breaks' are today. Future President Benjamin Franklin recalls in his diary how his first job as a print shop apprentice largely revolved around running to the nearest beer shop to keep his workmates supplied.

The early years of the colonies were not a great success in the eyes of the government back home, and it was decided that action was necessary to encourage expansion and therefore greater economic generation. In an effort to encourage new inhabitants to move to remote areas, representatives of the Crown soon directed each community to open a tavern or inn to service the needs of travellers. The scheme was a roaring success and, as in England, the tavern soon became the hub of the local community. From the 1680s, for instance, the tavern of John Turner hosted so many sessions of the Boston court that he actually designed one of its rooms to look like a court chambers.

The Crown also found beer was the perfect solution to another outstanding problem with its colonies. Unwilling to station standing armies, the British decided instead that each colony should provide its own part time militia. Unfortunately, the frontier farmers and traders couldn't be bothered with the hassle of assembling every week and training to become a fighting force. The problem was swiftly resolved when the Crown governors underwrote a few barrels of beer at the local tavern. Able-bodied militiamen suddenly appeared out of the woodwork to claim their free ale, and it wasn't long before 'Drill Day' was an unmissable social function of the North American frontier.

Ironically, it was beer that had a hand in causing the downfall of British colonial rule in America. For it was the same taverns that had become the social focus of disparate communities that also became the birthplace of political dissent from where revolution was plotted. Indeed it was from a tavern that an irate mob spilled out to provoke Boston's British garrison into what became known as 'the Boston Massacre'. From that moment, the fate of the British in the New World was sealed.

THE HARD STUFF – GIN MAKES AN APPEARANCE

Until the end of the 1600s, the Englishman's consumption of alcohol remained endearingly simple. For the masses, there was beer, cider and mead. For the slightly better off in society, there was a plentiful supply of European wine. In far-flung Ireland and Scotland, some of the locals were contentedly distilling highly potent grain-based spirits – but this was largely for their own consumption. Alcohol was a deeply entrenched part of life, but a largely inoffensive one. Spirits existed in the form of a crude distillate called aquavitae, and from a lucrative trade in smuggled French brandy.

All that was to change dramatically and ruinously in the last years of the 17th century when William of Orange came to the throne and promptly introduced English society to the latest craze of his native Holland: gin.

Originally developed in the early 17th century as a medicine to cure stomach complaints, gout and gallstones, the Dutch had turned the clear grain distillate into something a lot more palatable by adding juniper berries. Indeed it was the Dutch word for juniper, *genever*, which became the derivative for the word gin. The drink soon became a firm favourite of English soldiers fighting the 30 Years' War in the Low Countries, who found a drop of 'Dutch courage' did wonders to counter the damp conditions. They took it back to England and it found favour among the poor – but it was difficult to obtain. Ever since 1638, when a patent for distilling 'strong waters' had been granted to Sir Theodore Mayerne and Thomas Cadman of the Distillers' Company, there had been strict regulations about the methods and standard of distilling and in London there were just 200 establishments licensed to sell distilled alcohol.

William, however, celebrated his arrival on the English throne by passing a series of statutes actively encouraging the distillation of spirits. The distilling tax was abolished, as was the control on manufacturing standards. It meant that anyone could now distil by simply posting a notice in public and waiting for ten days.

It could be argued that the new king was doing his best for the rural economy by offering farmers an outlet for their surplus corn and barley. But what he actually unleashed upon the unsuspecting British was an unprecedented epidemic of drunkenness that very nearly brought the country to its knees. In the space of just 35 years from 1700, the consumption of gin on which excise duty had been paid shot up from half a million to five million gallons – and the amount of illicit gin consumed was probably ten times as much. Cheaply produced gin began to be distributed to workers as part of their wages, and soon the volume sold daily exceeded that of beer and ale, which was more expensive anyway. Such was the demand that many workers found themselves permanently in debt, owing most of their wages even before they got them.

Gin shops sprang up all over London, selling alcohol that had been distilled from anything that would ferment. A contemporary report declared that gin peddlers 'sell even in the streets and highways, some on bulks set up for that purpose and others in wheelbarrows, and many more who sell privately in garrets, cellars, backrooms and other places... All chandlers, many tobacconists and such who sell fruit and herbs in stalls sell geneva [gin], and many inferior tradesmen begin now to keep it in their shops for their customers.'

To the downtrodden masses, especially those forced to live in penury in London's increasingly cramped and squalid conditions, here was a cheap route to oblivion. 'Drunk for a penny, dead drunk for two-pence, clean straw for nothing' was the self-explanatory sales pitch, and horrendous contemporary illustrations of London streets, such as William Hogarth's *Gin Lane*, vividly show the appalling social consequences. Whole swathes of the capital's slumland became reeking ghettos. In a sobering precursor to modern-day heroin addiction, there are reports of gin addicts pawning all their possessions for their next gin. Others turned to robbery and murder. Lord Hervey was moved to declare, 'Drunkenness of the common people was universal, the whole town of London swarmed with drunken people from morning till night.' The numbers of deaths through gin consumption were in their thousands and, during the 30-year period when gin drinking was uncontrolled, the population of London fell drastically. There were twice as many burials as christenings, which included an inordinate number of babies who had been fed gin by their mothers in order to keep them quiet. In such squalid circumstances, gin justly deserved its nickname, 'mother's ruin'.

In 1726, with 7,000 shops in London solely dedicated to selling spirits and the average Londoner consuming a pint of gin a day, the Royal College of Physicians petitioned Parliament to do something about the growing menace. In 1736, the Gin Act was introduced, which made gin prohibitively expensive in a bid to curb consumption. But the fact the law took ten years to pass was indicative of the government's feeling that it would be largely unenforceable. They were right. Riots broke out and the law was routinely flouted. Around 11 million gallons of gin were produced every year in London alone, which was more than 20 times the 1690 figure and the equivalent of an eye-popping 14 gallons for each adult male. In two years, more than 12,000 people were convicted for offences against the new Act and, by 1742, gin production had increased by 50 per cent from the levels made just six years earlier. Furthermore there were so many loopholes in the Act that it was a simple matter to sell gin under a thin disguise. Gin shops now sold tots of exotic-sounding liquor such as 'Sangaree', 'Tow-row', 'Bob', 'Cuckold's Comfort', 'Ladies Delight' and 'King Theodore of Corsica', which were all gin. Meanwhile chemists' shops did a roaring trade in miraculous gin-based medicines.

There were also plenty of examples of entrepreneurial flair in evidence, as gin sellers did their best to make money from a greedy marketplace. One man is reported to have nailed a sign illustrating a cat to the ground floor window of his house. Under the cat's paw he fixed a lead pipe with a funnel at the end. Punters were invited to put their money in the cat's mouth and whisper 'Pussy, give me two-pennoth of gin', whereupon a tot would come gushing from the funnel. Other gin sellers took the logical step of peddling their wares in the prisons of London, Westminster and Southwark. In 1776 over 120 gallons of gin were being sold every week to the very inmates whose gin swilling had landed them behind bars in the first place.

The Gin Act, far from curbing the epidemic, had increased it. And its effects were being felt right across the country. Towns such as Bristol, Salisbury, Rochester and Manchester were reporting the same levels of anarchy, drunkenness and idleness as London.

For the beleaguered authorities, there was only one thing for it. The useless Gin Act was repealed and, in 1751 and 1756, punitive taxation and severe penalties for illegal distilling were introduced. By 1760, the tax on gin had reached the prohibitive figure of £24.50 ($36.07) per tun, which suited the government because it not only clamped down on the gin epidemic but also provided the Treasury with some welcome revenue. In the slums of London and elsewhere, the poor were forced back onto beer in order to blot out their miserable lives and, by the end of the century, gin consumption had slumped from eight million gallons a year to just one million.

ALTERNATIVE TOTS – WHISKY, VODKA, RUM

It is ironic that, while it was the English and their craze for gin that produced unrivalled scenes of social breakdown, it is the Scots, with their love for whisky, who are traditionally parodied as being helpless drunks. In fact whisky has a noble history that dates back to the days of the ancient Celts – the word itself is derived from *uisge-beatha*, meaning 'water of life' – and the drink has been treated by the Scots with a respect bordering on reverence.

While there is evidence to suggest that the art of distilling could have been taken to Scotland by early Christian missionary monks, the unique flavour of whisky is owed entirely to the blend of home-grown barley and Highland spring water. By the 17th century whisky was as essential a part of the Scottish diet as beer was to the English, and prompted one excise man to observe, 'The ruddy complexion, nimbleness and strength of these people is not owing to water-drinking, but to the aquavitae, a malt spirit which serves for both victual and drink.'

The same excise man would not have been waxing so lyrical about actually taxing the Scots for their aquavitae. The first attempts at controlling whisky production were made in 1664 when the Scots Parliament imposed a duty of 2p per gallon. It was cheerfully ignored by the Scots, who continued to produce their whisky in traditional home-made stills. Even after the Culloden massacre of 1746, when the clan system was broken up and the wearing of tartan forbidden, attempts to enforce whisky taxes and break up illicit stills continued to fail. The first officially sanctioned distilleries only came into being after 1823, when legal distilling was sanctioned at a reasonable duty of 12p per gallon for stills with a capacity of more than 40 gallons. Realising that it would be more profitable in the long term to pay tax but have unfettered access to the markets of Britain and abroad, increasing numbers of distillers went over to the right side of the law – and the Scottish whisky industry was born.

Some time in the mid-1300s, a British ambassador in Moscow woke up with an enormous hangover and pronounced vodka to be the national drink of Russia. The epithet stuck, and even today we do not think of vodka without imagining shovel-faced Slavs knocking back shooters of the hard stuff while muttering *'Dos vedanya'* to each other. But, although the drink derives from the Russian word *voda,* meaning water, it is the Poles who claim to be the inventors of vodka. They were making a crude distillation in the 8th century, some 100 years before the first documented production of vodka in Russia – although the Russians point out that because they used wine, the Poles were in fact making brandy. This argument does lose its impact, however, when you consider that vodka can be legitimately made from any fermentable raw material.

Whoever was first, it makes little difference. Early vodka would have been all but unpalatable to modern tastebuds, which savour the spirit for its purity above all. Indeed, like most early spirits, vodka was used primarily for medicinal purposes, as well as being an ingredient in the production of gunpowder! Production was crude: distillation was either by seasoning, ageing, freezing or even precipitation using the air bladders of sturgeons. To mask its horrible taste, the early vodka distillers used copious amounts of fruit, herbs and spices, and experimented with different source materials to achieve the perfect result, such as: absinthe, acorn, birch, chicory, sorrel, dill, horseradish, lemon, mint and watermelon. Such was the dedication and time required to produce decent vodka, production remained small-scale.

The first exports of Russian vodka were to Sweden in 1505, and from other eastern European countries during the course of the next century. It was not until the 19th century, however, that the drink began to gain a Europe-wide appeal thanks to the involvement of Russian soldiers in the Napoleonic wars. The escalating demand meant an increase in lower-grade products and vodka became predominantly based on distilled potato mash. This low-grade rocket fuel had the same effect on the Russian poor as gin had on the English a century before and, in 1894, in an effort to curb widespread urban drunkenness, the government brought in laws to make the production and distribution of vodka a state monopoly. It was only at the end of the 19th century, with all state distilleries adopting a standard production technique and hence a guarantee of quality, that the name vodka was officially and formally recognized.

This situation lasted only as long as it took for Lenin and the Bolsheviks to confiscate all the private distilleries in Moscow following the 1917 revolution. This prompted a number of leading vodka producers to flee the country, taking their skills and recipes with them. After a brief sojourn in France, one such exile set up the first vodka distillery in the USA in 1934, using the French version of his family name, Smirnoff. In the West, the popularity of vodka did not begin to take off until the 1960s and 1970s, when more brands began to be introduced into the UK and the USA. The affluent and experimental generation found vodka's 'mixability' highly desirable, and vodka cocktails became almost as numerous as gin. Today, thanks to the rise of alcopops and some clever marketing ploys, vodka is the fastest-growing category of major spirit drunk in the UK, while it is the biggest-selling spirit in the USA.

Unlike almost all traditional alcoholic drinks, rum was not originally a product of its natural surroundings. While Italy and France had the grapes, England the hops and Scotland the natural spring water, the West Indies had to wait until the late 15th century until the Spaniards introduced the cultivation of sugar cane required to make this rich, dark spirit. Once in place, however, the area never looked back and it is still the world's premier rum-producing area.

The earliest rum was a fearsome brew called variously 'Kill Devil' or 'rumbullion', and it was produced in Barbados in the early 17th century. Because of the maritime significance of the Caribbean, rum soon became the adopted drink of the various navies, merchantmen and pirates who dropped anchor off the islands – and it retained its strong affinity with naval tradition for centuries afterwards. In 1731, British sailors were given the choice of a daily pint of wine or half-pint of rum instead of their gallon ration of beer a day. Rum got its nickname 'grog' courtesy of Admiral Vernon – owner of a fine coat made of grogram, a coarse fabric made of silk and wool mixture – who in 1741 ordered the rum ration to be diluted with water. This was almost as popular as the decision in 1824 to cut the ration to quarter of a pint, and replace the rest with tea.

'WHITE MAN'S FIRE-WATER' – ALCOHOL AND WORLD DOMINATION
Wherever Europeans voyaged, they took their favourite tipple with them – and, if they were staying long, they also took the means to produce their favourite tipple. Hence the emergence of wine-producing vineyards in the

Americas, the Cape, Australia and New Zealand, and the spread of indigenous drinks like vodka, gin, beer and whisky to the furthest parts of the known world.

But wherever Europeans voyaged, they invariably tried to conquer and exploit – and history shows that alcohol had a vital and sordid part to play in both aims. Using brews that were invariably far stronger than anything the natives had ever tried, early colonists were able to weaken and suppress the indigenous population. The Romans, for example, were able to keep hold of most of their vast Empire by controlling the manufacture and supply of wine, literally keeping the savages docile by ensuring they were drunk. Some 1,500 years later, the same techniques were practised with equally cold-blooded calculation by the African slave traders and by the North American colonists.

The notorious triangular slave trade of the 18th century started with ships from English ports such as Bristol and Liverpool, which were heading for the west coast of Africa laden with liquor to be traded for Negro slaves. The slaves were then shipped, in the most appalling conditions imaginable, to the plantations of the West Indies where they were replaced in the hold by raw sugar cane and molasses. This was then taken back to England where it was distilled into the liquor required to finance another slaving voyage.

In North America, cheap and potent European liquor may have originally been used as a peace offering, but it soon became a tool for manipulation and exploitation by the first traders who saw its effects on the natives. For just a few sips of low-grade 'fire-water', the traders were rewarded with furs, food and even land. For the hopelessly addicted natives, the only reward within just a few short generations was ruin.

BREWING UP – ALCOHOL IN THE INDUSTRIAL AGE

With the menace of gin under control by the middle of the 18th century, Britain reverted back to its traditional obsession with beer, and for the next hundred years set about defining the product in all its glory. A rich and varied panoply of ales and beers was produced, with taste, colour and ingredients changing according to geography and topography. Many of the terms and references are still familiar today. In the south, a dark, strongly hopped beer was developed that was a great favourite of market porters and became known simply as porter. In Dublin, a rich black ale called stout was developed. In Burton-on-Trent, the predominant hard water helped produce a dry draught ale, strongly flavoured with hops, which was known as bitter.

At the end of the 18th century, perhaps inevitably, this small, highly individual cottage industry had begun to amalgamate into a series of larger breweries. Names like Whitbread and Guinness began to appear on beer casks. By 1815, fuelled by steam power, two million gallons – or a fifth of all beer production in Britain – was produced by just 11 breweries. 'Forty years ago, there was not a labourer in this parish that did not brew his own beer,' lamented one Sussex farmer in 1821. 'Now there is not one who does it.'

The redundant home brewers must have had a wry smile when, on 16 October 1814, one of London's leading breweries suffered a devastating – yet strangely bizarre – accident. On that day, an employee at the Meaux & Co Brewery was conducting his daily patrol of the site when he noticed a metal band on one of the giant wooden holding tanks appeared to be misaligned. He forgot all about it, but later that day the band snapped, bursting the 8m (26') high 4,000-barrel vat. Its contents slammed into the adjacent tank, rupturing it and sending a huge tidal wave of beer smashing through the brick walls of the brewery. Suddenly, the entire neighbourhood was engulfed in beer. In the nearby Tavistock Arms, drinkers were trapped when a river of the beer swept through the door and flooded the tap room, plunging the customers and the bar staff into the cellar. While most residents ran upstairs to avoid the beery deluge, some chose to take advantage of the situation by diving headlong into the torrent. When the foam cleared, the death toll of people crushed by the tidal wave numbered 12, while 8 more were found dead of what investigators later described as 'death by alcohol coma'.

Still, despite the expansion of industrial brewing, there was plenty of variety to be had compared to the handful of multi-national concerns that control the global brewing industry today. And, in global terms, the first half of the 19th century was a golden age of alcohol consumption in general.

On both sides of the Atlantic, people were boozing in copious amounts. In 1840s England, the *per capita* spirit consumption was even higher than it had been during the dark days of the gin craze. And beer, having undergone a slump at the beginning of the century, was again up to a hearty 34.4 gallons per head in 1876.

Elsewhere in Europe, meanwhile, it was the Germans who were beginning to set down their standard in the brewing industry. In cities like Munich, disparate home brewers had begun to club together to form the first brewing conglomerates, and they were able to set the market price for their product. There was an eager market: beer drinking was nudging the 40 gallons per head mark by the mid-1800s.

The industrial revolution had even touched on the traditional and ancient art of wine making. In France, Italy and Spain, vineyard owners discovered that it was now possible to produce vast quantities of wine without affecting the distinctive regional flavours or, most importantly, offending the drinking public. Indeed, improved wine-making techniques made it possible to actually improve the vintage in many cases, and exports were soaring.

The same was true in eastern Europe, where the thirst for vodka could be sated much more easily and safely through industrial processes. The days of the lone distiller were numbered, as the Russian authorities realized that by building and operating vodka factories it was possible to exert far more control over the often unruly populace than it was through traditional means of taxation.

But as beer and wine sales rocketed, spirit sales began to tumble. If ever a product needed re-branding it was gin, and in the 19th century that is exactly what happened in the shape of 'gin palaces'. Set up initially by the distillers as a means of fighting back against the beer brewing industry, gin palaces were gaudy, expensively decorated bars that were a million miles from the seedy gin shops of a hundred years before. They became a social centre, attracting the well heeled and the well-to-do and at the same time repositioning gin as a tipple for the educated middle classes.

A typical gin palace was described in 1836 by Charles Dickens in his *Sketches By Boz*:

'The gay building with a fantastically ornamental parapet, the illuminated clock, the plate-glass windows surrounded by stucco rosettes and its profusion of gas lights in richly gilt burners, is perfectly dazzling when contrasted with the darkness and dirt we have just left. A bar of french-polished mahogany, elegantly carved, extends the whole width of the place; there are two aisles of great casks, painted green and gold, enclosed with a light brass rail and bearing such descriptions as 'Old Tom', 'Young Tom', 'Samson'...'

Such opulence served to improve gin's tarnished image – but in Britain beer remained king. For a start, vastly improved brewing techniques had made it far safer to drink than ordinary water. It was also cheaper by volume than coffee or tea. But what really helped was the Sale of Beer Act 1830, which made it legal for anyone to sell beer as long as they paid an excise fee of two guineas. The thinking behind the Act was, according to the government, to provide an alternative to the gin shop and 'give the poor and working classes of the community the chance of obtaining a better, cheaper and more wholesome beverage'. They hoped that the Act, which also proposed to abolish duty on beer, would lead to more competition that would in turn lead to better-quality beer that was free from adulteration.

Alcohol sponsorship is extremely prevalent in the USA and UK and has many critics, but it is a less sensitive issue in the rest of Europe where there is far less sponsorship in sport and the sums involved are generally considerably smaller.

Prime Minister the Duke of Wellington considered the Beer Act to be the greatest achievement of his long and illustrious career – but it was as if the country had learned nothing from William of Orange's disastrous decision to open up the gin market. In Liverpool, 50 new 'beer-houses' were opened every day for 6 weeks. By the end of 1830 there were 24,000 beer-houses in England and Wales, and almost 50,000 five years later. As the beer-houses fought for custom with the more established inns and taverns, beer was routinely adulterated to make watered down ale seem stronger. And far from this cheaper beverage encouraging 'wholesome'

Gary Marshall, landlord of the Blisland Inn in Blisland near Bodmin, Cornwall, after his pub won CAMRA's (the Campaign for Real Ale) award for Pub Of The Year, 2001.

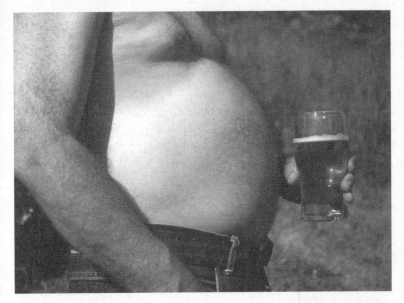

Regular beer drinkers are commonly overweight, due to the significant contribution of alcohol to the energy content of their diet.

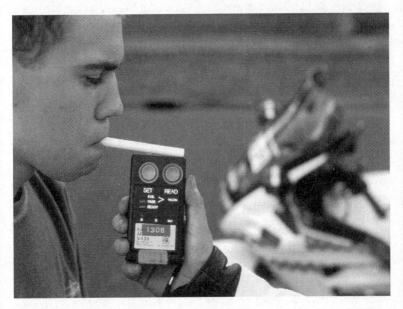

A motorist taking an alcohol breath test at the side of a road after being suspected of drink-driving. The breathalyzer he is blowing into gives an on-the-spot indication of whether the amount of alcohol in his bloodstream is above the legal limit.

citizens, beer-houses became dens of iniquity where gambling, prostitution and cruel sports were practised with vigour. Again it took an inordinate amount of time for the law to be repealed – 40 years in this case – by which time beer-houses were spreading at the rate of 2,000 a year. The 1869 Wine and Beer-house Act made it necessary to obtain a magistrate's licence to open a new beer-house, and ten years later the beer duty was reintroduced. Happy days of free beer had come to an end.

FIGHT FOR THE RIGHT TO PARTY – BEER WARS

Sadly, the sight of beer-fuelled football yobs on the rampage in picturesque town squares has become all-too-common in the latter part of the 20th century. But while not defending the drunken antics of a deranged minority, it is true that throughout history alcohol has been the catalyst for the kind of inner-city riot that makes the Barmy Army look like Girl Guides on a weekend field trip.

In 1715, for instance, the conflict between the James II-supporting Jacobites and the Royalist Hanoverians was at full cry. In London, the Hanoverians organized themselves into loose associations that gathered in back-street taverns in order to foment plans against the rebels. These meetings became known as Mug House Clubs. On 31 October, probably more by design than accident, a group of Jacobites entered the same Mug House as the Hanoverians and a slanging match broke out that soon exploded into full-blooded fighting. The scrapping spilled out into the streets and into other Mug Houses and continued unabated for several days, causing a number of fatalities and thousands of pounds of damage. The incidents were dubbed the Mug House Riots.

In 1848, beer lit the spark that led to a vicious and deadly riot in Munich, Germany. In the 1840s, the alcohol industry was dominated by a small cartel of brewers who, in an attempt to control the market, engaged in some pretty blatant price fixing. In 1848, when the price of beer was raised by one penny, the ale-loving people of Munich had had enough. A mob of angry protesters marched on the Spaten brewery, where they met an equally determined and heavily armed military presence. Fighting broke out, gunfire erupted and, when the smoke cleared, dozens of protesters lay dead.

The same city saw yet more beer rebellion in 1995 – although thankfully this protest passed off peacefully. On this occasion, more than 20,000 demonstrators brought Munich to a standstill when they marched in protest at the government's plan to regulate the hours of the city's famous beer gardens. A petition exceeding 200,000 signatures was handed over, and the plans were shelved.

In the USA, lawmen like Wyatt Earp made a name for themselves by clamping down on the excesses of the lawless frontier towns of the Wild West. Dodge City, in particular, was a den of hard drinking that inevitably erupted into violence at regular intervals. Yet the most notorious beer riot in American history occurred not in some one horse town in Kansas but rather in comparatively sophisticated Chicago.

In the mid-19th century, the Windy City was run by a proto-Fascist 'Americans-only' faction who had managed to cash in on ethnic rivalry by getting their candidate Dr Levi Boone elected mayor. Boone hated the German and Irish immigrants with a passion, resenting the way they had formed their own neighbourhoods, churches and trade unions. Most of all, though, Boone hated their passion for beer, which he considered to be an un-American evil. In 1855, he set about making their lives miserable.

Boone's plan was simple. He increased liquor licence fees by 600 per cent and coupled this with a three-month moratorium on issuing licences. Next, he ordered a re-enactment of an old law prohibiting alcohol and beer sales on Sunday. To reinforce the point, on the first Sunday of enforcement his militia went into the predominantly German and Irish quarter of the city and arrested more than 200 beer drinkers.

But Boone had underestimated the effect this beer ban would have. On the day of the trial, an angry 300-strong mob descended on Courthouse Square. After a series of tense stand offs, violence erupted and several people on both sides were killed. Panic stricken by how this would appear, Boone immediately ceased his campaign. But the damage was done: the Germans and the Irish were able to return to their Sunday afternoon beer, and Boone and his party quickly faded from the political scene. Today, Chicago is regarded as one of America's great beer-drinking cities – due in no small part to the so-called Chicago Lager Beer Riots.

As if to prove that alcohol abuse can have deleterious effects on the animal kingdom as well as the human race, in 1996 a herd of elephants in India broke into a rural hut and consumed a batch of potent homebrew. Drunk, they went on the rampage and killed several villagers.

JUST SAY NO – THE TEMPERANCE MOVEMENT

Temperance was not a new idea. More than 1,500 years before the seemingly unthinkable concept of abstinence swept across the USA and Europe, the Prophet Mohammed outlawed alcohol for millions of Moslems in the East, and it was frowned upon by different religious sects around the world.

While many may shiver at the very idea today, in reality the Temperance Movement was a highly logical, not to mention inevitable, result of some quite breathtaking levels of alcoholic excess in the years leading up to its formation. Similarly, the enthusiasm with which it was adopted says more about the ruinous state of society than about the missionary zeal of the Temperance members themselves.

Temperance began in America in the late 18th century and soon spread to Europe – although it is important to note that it was only spirits, not beer, that was the enemy originally. Beer was still perceived as a dietary staple.

There was much to be done. We have seen the effects of gin on an English sub-class supposedly governed by laws and lawmakers; in America's 'Wild' West, where literally anything went, it is easy to imagine how hard liquor came to affect the remote communities dotted across the frontier. The old-style movie images of saloon-bar slug-fests, rootin'-tootin' gunfights and cowpokes so drunk they can no longer stand were romanticized – but not by much. All of this was anathema to the waspish citizens of the continent's east coast, who saw all of their hard work in establishing the United States as a viable concern in the world being eroded by the drunken excesses of the rowdy west. Although the earliest Temperance Movement had been formed in upstate New York as early as 1808, it was not until 1826 that the American Temperance Society (ATS) was inaugurated in Boston. It immediately became a powerful force, co-ordinating a growing nationwide campaign against spirit drinking. Within nine years, the ATS had over 1.5 million members – or about one in five of the 'free' population.

Although the clergy and the medical profession were at the forefront of the organization, its core lay in a strong lay community. Such was the success of the ATS in persuading people to lay off the spirits, that the organization was soon arguing that true temperance meant abstinence from all alcoholic drink. This position was given the name 'teetotalism' because those who signed the new total pledge had the letter T entered by their names.

Inevitably, there were splinter groups who believed in taking the message further. One such group, calling themselves the Washingtonians, was formed in Baltimore in the 1840. Very much a precursor of Alcoholics Anonymous, the Washingtonians believed in helping reformed drunks and announced its arrival in towns across the US with spectacular torchlit processions and lively public meetings. Within two years, they had claimed to have 'saved at least 100,000 common drunkards and three times that number of tipplers who were on a fair way to becoming sots'.

The startling success of the Temperance Movement was such that it soon began to have an impact on the political scene, and individual states were keen to be seen to be promoting the message. In 1851, Maine introduced draconian laws prohibiting the production of alcohol within the state, limited selling rights to state agencies and also introduced heavy fines and imprisonment for anyone flouting the law. When riots broke out, the state militia was ordered to fire on the crowd and one demonstrator was killed. Despite this, other states clamoured to introduce similar legislation, so that, by 1855, the 13 states had introduced prohibition – a word that would come back to haunt America 65 years later.

'The most plausible explanation for the toughness of the American reaction to alcohol during the first half of the 19th century must be that when a society feels itself insulted and endangered by the damage which it perceives drink to be causing, a society may turn against alcohol completely,' notes Griffith Edwards, Emeritus Professor of Addiction at the University of London.

Ireland was the first European country to follow the American lead, with the tiny village of Skibbereen being credited as the home of the first temperance society. In Wexford, members signed a pledge in which they agreed 'to refrain from the use of distilled spirits, except as medicine in the case of bodily ailment; that we will not allow the use of them in our families, nor provide them for the entertainment of our friends, and that we will, in all suitable ways, discountenance the use of them in the community at large'. In Belfast, Dr John Edgar celebrated the launch of the Ulster Temperance Society in 1829 by pouring all of his whisky out of the window and into the courtyard below.

The great hero of the Irish Temperance Movement was a thin, weedy fellow called Father Theobald Mathew – who many cynics said looked as if he could do with a drink to put a bit of colour in his cheeks. Nevertheless, he was possessed of amazing oratorical skills allied with a missionary zeal against the demon drink. At packed halls and open-air venues, he would engage the crowd in a rowdy question-and-answer session: 'What does a racehorse drink? Water! What does the elephant drink? Water! What does the lion drink? Water!'. Even in the booziest slums in Ireland, Mathew had the ability to empty the pubs and the drinking dens and persuade thousands of people to take his pledge of abstinence. In just three months in 1838, it is claimed that 25,000 had taken the pledge, and that figure shot up to nearly 200,000 by the end of the year (although the official statistics were almost certainly massaged by Mathew's supporters). What is not in doubt is that during Mathew's preaching peak, in 1838–42, consumption of spirits in Ireland fell from 12.3 million gallons (56 million litres) to just 5.3 million (25 million litres). Breweries and ale-houses went out of business, drunkenness dropped, and even the crime rate fell. Mathew had similar success during his lightning raids across the Irish Sea to the mainland. In one six-week tour, he is reported to have signed up 600,000

> Because temperance writers insisted that alcohol was a poison, they demanded that school books never mentioned the contradictory fact that physicians commonly prescribed alcohol for health and medicinal purposes. Similarly, because the temperance movement taught that drinking alcohol was sinful, it was forced to confront the contrary fact that Jesus drank wine. Its solution was to insist that Jesus really drank grape juice. During Prohibition, temperance activists hired a scholar to remove all references to alcoholic beverages within the Bible.

people. How many of these converts actually remained teetotallers is a different matter, however. On his death in 1856, a statue of Mathew was erected in Dublin with its back deliberately turned to the numerous grog shops that were once again doing a roaring trade.

In Scotland and England, the temperance banner was taken up with equal gusto. In 1830, the Scottish Temperance Movement claimed 130 societies and 25,000 members. Across the border, societies were founded in every major city. In London, the British and Foreign Temperance Society was formed, with the Bishop of London as its president and Queen Victoria as its patron. But, as in the USA, certain factions were not content simply with abstinence from spirits. In Lancashire, seven members of the Preston Temperance Society signed a pledge that read, 'We agree to abstain from all liquors of an intoxicating quality, whether ale, porter, wine or ardent spirits, except as medicine.' Similar groups, such as the Independent Order of Rechabites, preached the total abstinence mantra: 'Malt not, brew not, distil not, buy not, sell not, drink not'. The Band of Hope was formed in 1847 for children under 16, which provided singing, sightseeing excursions and camping trips for youngsters prepared to pledge, 'I do agree that I will not use intoxicating liquors as a beverage.' By the end of the century, it had more than three million members. Meanwhile Thomas Cook, who formed a highly successful travel agency still around today, spread the temperance message by ferrying teetotallers up and down the country to attend meetings and marches at venues such as the Great Exhibition of 1851.

It was around this time that the British Temperance Movement split into two distinct and warring factions: the 'moral persuasionists', who aimed to beat drink by getting everyone to sign the pledge; and the 'prohibitionists', who were greatly impressed by the activities across the Atlantic in Maine. In 1853 this latter group formed an organization called The United Kingdom Alliance (for the Suppression of the Traffic in all Intoxicating Liquors), with a firebrand leader called John B Gough. They demanded a total ban on alcohol. This fundamentalism unnerved the moral persuasionists, and led to an outbreak of bad blood. The schism between the two groups was highlighted when the moral persuasionists tried to discredit Gough in a court case that claimed he took drink and drugs himself.

By the mid-1850s it seemed that internecine strife, coupled with a decrease in popular anxiety about alcohol, had derailed the Temperance Movement on both sides of the Atlantic. In England, the movement was dealt a serious blow when the 1854 Sale of Beer Act, which had seriously restricted Sunday opening hours, was repealed shortly after a series of popular riots and demonstrations. And in 1859 a prototype prohibition bill was overwhelmingly defeated in the Commons – largely due to the prospect of losing the vast alcohol tax that amounted to almost a third of the national budget.

Across the Atlantic, the hastily introduced prohibition laws were by now being routinely flouted and enforcement had become largely non-existent. But for the American Temperance Movement, the cavalry was about to come charging over the hill in the most unexpected of circumstances.

In December 1873, saloon owners and liquor sellers in Washington DC were astonished to find their premises being picketed by a gang of women demanding that they break open their casks and pour the contents down the drain. The women were led by community activist Bethia Ogle, and their technique of alternately haranguing and threatening drink shops proved spectacularly successful and soon the gutters of the capital were running with hooch. Ogle, along with a number of other female activists, were the catalyst for the Woman's Christian Temperance Union (WCTU) formed later that same year under the formidable leadership of Mrs Frances E Willard. With Willard at the helm, the WCTU began a no-holds-barred assault on alcohol, demonizing it as poison and flooding the nation with pamphlets. Willard even managed to get the views of the WCTU accepted onto school syllabuses, and teaching on the evils of alcohol became mandatory across most of America. 'The traditional defenders of peaceful home life felt so emotionally agitated by [alcohol] that the movement developed with unprecedented passion and spontaneity,' notes Jancis Robinson.

The rise of the WCTU coincided and overlapped with that of the Prohibition Party, which, by putting forward a presidential candidate (the former mayor of prohibitionist Maine), first offered up prohibition as a national political issue in 1880. The fact that they also campaigned for universal suffrage, equal pay for women and the abolition of the death penalty contributed in no small means to their crushing defeat – but the ball was rolling. In 1893, the Anti-Saloon League, which campaigned solely for the abolition of bawdy and boozy drinking houses, succeeded in attracting a wide range of support, from both organized labour and employers and, by the outbreak of World War I, was sufficiently established to have its call for total prohibition taken seriously. When America entered the war in 1917, the League used its influence to secure the passage, by Congress, of a bill banning the use of grain for distilling. In the interests of conserving vital food stocks for the unknown future, this made perfect sense. But in December of the same year, Congress agreed to submit to the vote of individual states a proposal for national prohibition. If the League were over the moon about this development, they must have been ecstatic when, the following year, Congress voted for complete prohibition for the length of the war. The die was cast: in January 1919, two months after the war ended, individual state legislatures began voting on whether they should support the Volstead Act, which proposed national prohibition; in January 1920 the Act became the 18th Amendment, was finally ratified and the era of Prohibition officially began.

NOT A DROP TO DRINK? – PROHIBITION, USA

Two contemporary quotes sum up the 13-year American Prohibition Era. The first, from the US Prohibition Commissioner: 'This law will be obeyed in cities, large and small, and in villages, and where it is not obeyed it will be enforced. The law says that liquor to be used as a beverage must not be manufactured. Not sold nor given away, nor hauled in anything on the surface of the earth nor in the air.' And this, from comedian Groucho Marx: 'I was TT (teetotal) until Prohibition.'

In one year of Prohibition, the citizens of the United States consumed 200 million gallons of malt liquor and 118 million gallons of wine, while the professional bootleggers earned themselves an income of $400 billion (£271.7 billion).

During the period of Prohibition there were over 700 gangland assassinations and almost 350,000 small timers arrested for drink offences, who were sentenced to a total of 33,000 years in prison. More than 35,000 people died from drinking poisonous liquor and many more were permanently incapacitated. In Chicago alone, drink-drive convictions rose by 475 per cent, and deaths from alcoholism by 600 per cent.

That Prohibition was one of the most ill conceived and misguided social policies of the 20th or any other century is beyond doubt. Quite how it ended up that way is a model example of what happens when governments are influenced by minority pressure groups and fail to heed the lessons of the past. It is also perhaps the defining moment in alcohol's history – the moment that proved its total and utter hold over human society, to the extent that, for 13 years, most Americans would have happily destroyed the fabric of their society rather than lose their drink.

At the root of the Prohibition problem was the fact that history had already proven that banning drink was about as effective as trying to hold back the tide. In the 1700s, as we have seen, the reaction to the gin clampdown in England was widespread riots and a thriving black market in illicit homebrew. Similarly, attempts by English excise men to control the whisky output of Scotland were derisively evaded. For the American government to think for one minute it would be able to enforce a total and nationwide ban on alcohol in 1920 shows staggering naivety and spinelessness in the face of influential pressure groups like the Anti-Saloon League.

What made matters worse is that the Volstead Act was fundamentally flawed to begin with. Quite simply, it was unenforceable. It was 'an act to prohibit intoxicating beverages', and criminalized only the commercial manufacture, sale and transport of intoxicating drink. What it *didn't* criminalize was the possession of alcohol, or the brewing of it in the home. As Griffith Edwards (Emeritus Professor of Addiction at the University of London) points out, 'The Volstead Act was not root-and-branch criminalization of alcohol, and no-one was going to be subjected to a street stop and search for alcohol, or be busted for keeping a bottle of bourbon in the closet... The degree of control was closer to the level found in relation to cannabis in those present-day jurisdictions which have decriminalized that drug and allowed personal possession than to the usual degree of criminal control exerted by modern-day societies in relation to heroin or cocaine.'

Even if Volstead had allowed for draconian street searches, such a policy would have been impossible to implement. There were barely enough federal agents to go round – a fact not helped by the fact that 30 were murdered in the first three years of Prohibition – and underfunding was chronic. Of those agents in service, more than 750 were dismissed between 1920 and 1926 for offences including extortion, bribery, illegal disposal of liquor, assault, theft and making false reports. Those who were 'straight down the line' were not much better. Over 1,000 civilians were gunned down by trigger-happy agents during the 13 years the Volstead Act was in force, including the senator for Vermont.

Even without such intrinsic faults, Volstead would have undoubtedly been undone by the desire of the general public to get a drink, and the ingenuity of the bootleggers willing to supply them. Warning of what was to come was served when, in the three months leading up to the implementation of the 18th Amendment, liquor worth $500,000 (£340,000) was stolen from government warehouses in readiness for the impending drought. In 1923, nearly a million gallons of wine were supposedly booked out for 'ecclesiastical' use in northern Illinois alone. In 1927, in response to the regulation that allowed every doctor to fill out 100 prescriptions for medicinal whisky in any three-month period, ailing Americans sloshed 1.8 million gallons of 'medicinal' hooch. In 1921, 96,000 illicit bootleg distilleries were seized; by 1930 the figure was 280,000. Production of 'near-beer' and industrial alcohol provided a loophole through which drink was made available, as did home-produced fermented fruit juice. Grape growers, meanwhile, were all too pleased to supply the market with a type of grape jelly called 'Vine-Go' that, with the addition of water, could make strong wine in just two months. Despite this rampant and blatant law breaking, the courts convicted less than seven per cent of those charged with liquor offences.

Prohibition immediately opened the door to organized crime. Until then, gang bosses in New York and Chicago had been comparatively petty criminals, content to run numbers rackets and evade taxes. After 1920, however, the scope for profiteering was literally boundless. Mobsters controlled a $40 million-a-year (£27.2 million) booze-smuggling business that involved routes from Europe, South America and Canada, and the

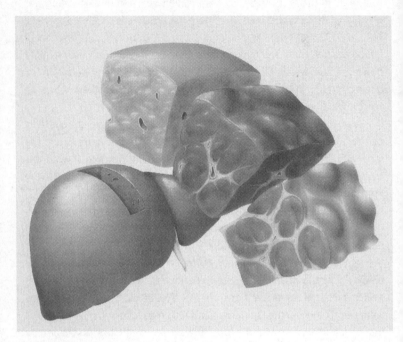

Artwork showing the development alcohol-induced liver cirrhosis. The liver is at lower left, with the cirrhosis developing in the liver sections from upper left to lower right. In cirrhosis, bands of fibrosis (internal scarring) break up the internal structure of the liver. The surviving cells multiply to form regeneration nodules separated by scar tissue (white). This gives a cirrhotic liver a granulated look. Heavy alcohol consumption is the most common cause of cirrhosis in developed countries. Symptoms include mild jaundice, œdema (swelling), mental confusion, and the vomiting of blood.

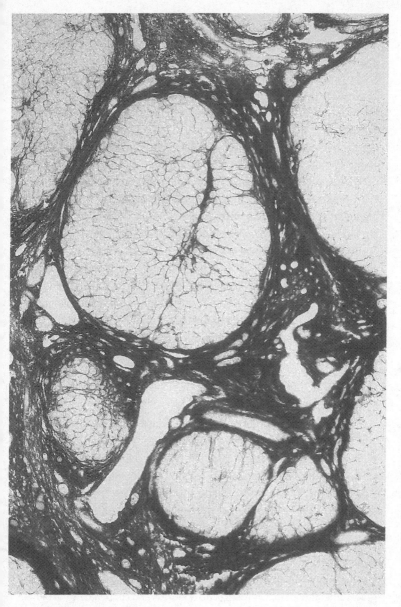

Light micrograph of a section through liver tissue showing alcohol-induced liver cirrhosis. Fibrous scar tissue has developed around oval liver lobules.

speakeasies – illegal drinking dens – that earned them even more. This is why, in Detroit, mafia boss Chester Le Mare was able to gross a staggering $215 million (£146 million) from his bootlegging activities *in one year.*

'In its practical effects,' notes Andrew Sinclair in his *Prohibition: The Era Of Excess*, 'national Prohibition transferred $2 billion (£1.36 billion) a year from the hands of brewers, distillers and shareholders to the hands of murderers, crooks and illiterates.'

Perhaps most tellingly of all, considering how Prohibition came about in the first place, the period of 1920–33 saw an almost terminal decline in the membership of temperance groups. And, just a few years after the ground-breaking campaigning of Mrs Frances E Willard and the Women's Christian Temperance Union, not only were increasing numbers of women drinking heavily and publicly during Prohibition, but the Women's Organization for National Prohibition Reform was founded, stating that Prohibition was 'wrong in principle', and 'disastrous in consequences in the hypocrisy, the corruption, the tragic loss of life and the appalling increase of crime which has attended the abortive attempt to enforce it.'

Drinking at an earlier age was also reported, particularly during the first few years of Prohibition. In 1926, one psychiatric hospital noted, 'During the past year, an unusually large group of patients who are of high school age were admitted for alcoholic psychosis.'

By 1932, the American public were so sick of Prohibition that any politician prepared to promise its repeal was guaranteed a landslide victory. That year Democratic nominee Franklin D Roosevelt stood before his party's National Convention in Chicago and announced, 'I congratulate this Convention for having had the courage fearlessly to write into its declaration of principles what an overwhelming majority here assembled really thinks about the 18th Amendment. This Convention wants repeal. Your candidate wants repeal. And I am confident that the United States of America wants repeal.'

The gun was cocked at Prohibition's temple. On 14 February 1933, the repeal amendment was introduced to Congress and approved by the Senate two days later. In June, Roosevelt and the Democrats swept into power with the slogan 'A New Deal and a pot of beer for everyone!' On 5 December

1933, Congress officially adopted the 21st Amendment to the Constitution, and a few days later Roosevelt himself tasted one of the first beers to be sold legally in the USA for 13 years.

In a speech given in 1931, US anatomist Florence Sabin claimed the Prohibition Act, 'written for weaklings and derelicts, has divided the nation, like Gaul, into three parts – wets, drys and hypocrites.'

But did 'America's nightmare' accomplish anything else, anything *positive*? Is there *anything* that can salvage Prohibition from the scrapheap of history? Well, it dispensed with the wholly undesirable saloon bar – thus fulfilling the original aim of the Anti-Saloon League in 1913. And, while speakeasies were illegal, they at least welcomed women through their doors, ushering in the era of the mixed sex cocktail bar.

More importantly, perhaps, the horrors of Prohibition killed off the Temperance Movement on both sides of the Atlantic for good. Instead of a black or white argument, people were able to decide for themselves how much or how little they wanted to drink. It is no surprise that as soon as Prohibition was lifted, alcohol consumption across the USA plummeted, bottoming out at a level that is largely the same as it is today. For the first time, people were learning to *live* with alcohol and, having seen both sides of excess, learning to respect it.

PROHIBITION – THE UK MISSES THE WAGON

At the end of the 19th century, UK prohibitionists could have been forgiven for thinking the Almighty was on their side when, to the horror of the wine industry, vineyards across Europe were systematically destroyed first by the fungal parasite oidium and then the plant louse phylloxera. It was not until 1920 that the great wine plague was eventually eradicated by grafting European vines onto American stocks, but with the Prohibition Movement gathering pace in the USA the omens looked good on the other side of the Atlantic, too.

However, it was not to be. Wherever it attempted to impart the wisdom of abstinence, the UK Temperance Movement found itself bashing its head against brick walls. In the 1860s, Gladstone and his Liberal Party were sympathetic to the temperance cause, but found themselves kicked out of office and replaced by the pro-brewing industry Conservatives. In 1908, they campaigned for a reduction in the number of pubs, famously recounting the tale of the working man who had to pass 20 public houses on his way home from work; on pay day, he passed 19, but could not resist the last one and blew all his family's money on beer. The resulting Liberal Licensing Bill passed through the Commons, but was blown out of the water by the Lords – whose Conservative members were still in the thrall of the brewing industry.

As with the US Prohibition Party, it was the outbreak of World War I that presented the UK Temperance Movement with its big chance. Initially, things looked bleak: wartime camaraderie lent itself to sing-songs down the pub, while it was the done thing to buy a brave soldier a pint (one decorated soldier from Lincoln returned from the Front to find 120 pints in the pump waiting for him, while three convalescent squaddies from Sheffield were treated so royally they were found unconscious on the tramlines). But, gradually, as the war dragged on and failed to be over by Christmas, the mood of the nation became more introspective. People decided it was not such a good idea to send their brave lads across to France with stinking hangovers, and it was certainly no good to the war effort if the munitions and shipyard workers were taking time off with drink-related illness.

The government, under Lloyd George, was quick to act. Opening hours in military and naval districts were restricted, a move which spread to half the country by the end of 1914. 'Treating' squaddies to a pint became an offence. And when the Prime Minister announced that 'Drink is doing more damage in the war than all the German submarines put together; we are fighting Germany, Austria and drink – and the greatest of these deadly foes is drink,' the Temperance Movement must have thought it was now only a matter of time before booze was banned altogether.

To their horror, Lloyd George merely diluted the beer and increased the duty on it by a halfpenny per half pint, thereby giving himself the best of both worlds: increased revenue to fund the war, and a reasonably peaceful – and sober – general public back home. 'Drink the national beverage and help your country!' trumpeted the advertisements. 'Order a pint of beer and drive a nail into the Kaiser's coffin! If you can't manage a pint, order a half and drive in a tin-tack!'

Stunned by this, the prohibitionists attempted one last counterblast before the end of the war. Picking up on the inevitable food shortage in Britain, they launched a new campaign attacking the 'waste' of cereal in beer. 'Bread before beer' was the catchy slogan – but the response was as lightweight as the campaign. Beer production had already been reduced from a pre-war 36 million barrels to 26 million in 1916; when they tentatively suggested reducing it by a further 10 million barrels in 1917 there was widespread dissent. Instead, the idea was quietly back-burnered, and the government decided to approve the brewing of a further six million gallons (27.3 million litres) of watered-down beer.

By the end of World War I, the Temperance Movement in the UK was a busted flush. Statistics showed that, in fact, alcohol consumption in 1918 was down by almost half from 1914 levels, alcohol-related crimes had slumped by two-thirds and alcohol-related deaths by five-sixths. Stumped and beaten, by 1920 the prohibitionists could only fire envious glances at the new regime across the pond and imagine how things might have been. In fact, as we've seen, events in the USA were about to kill off temperance forever.

WE'LL MEET AGAIN – ALCOHOL IN WORLD WAR II

Compared to World War I, there was very little hand-wringing about the effect of alcohol on the military or the workforce at home during the 1939–45 conflict. Chance would be a fine thing. Alcoholic drink of any description was in pitiful supply during the war and for a good decade after it. Spirits were severely rationed and available only through black market spivs, or 'under the counter' deals with friendly sources. The continental wine-importing business was non-existent and took years to build up again. Beer was, to some palates, even worse than the watered-down Lloyd George brew had been 30 years before.

> 'Alcohol is a good preservative for everything but brains.'
>
> – Mary Pettibone Poole

There are a million and one reasons why it is stupid to drink alcohol, why every time we bring a glass to our lips we take our life in our hands and put someone else's at risk. More than any other substance we choose to put into our body, other than perhaps cigarette smoke, alcohol is the most graphically and fervently vilified by those who oppose its consumption. To them, there is nothing that is good about alcohol – and even the factors that could be viewed as good are bad, as far as they are concerned. Alcohol is the demon drink, mother's ruin, the scourge of society, and the root of all evil. It both depresses us and unleashes our repressed thoughts. It rots our innards and it destroys our brains. It makes us violent and incoherent.

But hang on – isn't this the same stuff that has been proven to reduce cardiovascular disease, relieve stress in a wide range of age groups as well as provide calories without the fat, and several trace elements such as copper that, though essential for the smooth running of the heart, are in short supply in convenience diets? Isn't alcohol the substance that can provide zinc, manganese, potassium and many vitamins of the B group? Does it not lend itself to many positive aspects of our culture and history?

Yes, yes and yes to it all. Alcohol comes in many forms and levels of consumption, and whether it is 'good' or 'bad' for us depends largely on what, and how much, we drink.

WHAT IS ALCOHOL?

C_6H_5OH. Or at least that is the chemical formula for ethyl alcohol, aka ethanol, the only member of the alcohol family fit to drink. (The family also includes the poisonous methanol, glycerol, lactic acid, sorbitol and higher alcohols that are used in solvents.) C_6H_5OH is used in perfumes and even as a substitute for petrol. But it is as the basis of all alcoholic drinks that it is most loved and hated.

The following equation – $C_6H_{12}O_6 \rightarrow C_6H_5OH + CO_2$ – is the basic formula for turning sugar into alcohol and gas that has sustained humans ever since they first drank fermented fruit 12,000 years ago. Although the theory has changed little in the intervening years, the variety of uses to which it has been put most certainly has.

Wine was almost certainly the first alcoholic drink made, simply because it is the easiest to produce. The dusty bloom on the skin of a wine grape contains yeast; and, once a grape is crushed, the natural sugar inside comes into contact with this yeast. Assuming the temperature is high enough, this causes the process of fermentation to begin. Yeast then continues to work until all the sugar has been transformed into alcohol and carbon dioxide. The strength of the final product can be altered either by stopping the fermentation process in its tracks, or by adding sugar to the unfermented grape to give the yeast more to work on. Wines usually have an alcohol content of between 12 and 14 per cent. When the wine is fortified by the addition of extra alcohol, drinks such as sherry, port and Madeira are produced.

Cider (fermented apple juice), and its pear-based counterpart perry, are produced in the same way as wine, which explains why they have been a staple drink in non-grape producing countries such as England and Normandy for centuries. Their alcohol content varies from 3–12 per cent.

Beer, although almost as venerable, is a more complicated process because it is not simply made up of fermented barley and water. For a start, barley contains unfermentable starch rather than sugar, and compared to

> There's no worm in tequila but there is one in mescal, a spirit beverage that is distilled from a different plant. Actually it isn't specifically a worm but a butterfly caterpillar (*hipopta agavis*) called a gusano.

grapes is bland and tasteless. Various methods are employed to break down the starch. Some cultures, especially in South America and the South Pacific, chew the barley in order to release salivary enzymes. Thankfully, perhaps, western brewers choose to allow the grain to germinate slightly, thereby producing natural enzymes that break down the starch. Germination is then stopped by drying out the grain, and the resulting substance – called malt – is roasted to give it colour and flavour. Malt is then soaked in warm water to transform the starch into a fermentable mixture of glucose and maltose called wort. Hops is added to the wort to give it flavour, and the resulting non-alcoholic gloop is then ready for fermentation with specially developed yeasts that determine whether the final beverage is a light ale or lager, or traditional beer.

Yeast in its natural state tends to stop working when the alcohol content in a liquid reaches 14 or 15 per cent. In order to reach the whopping percentages present in spirits like whisky, gin and vodka a whole new, man-made science is required: distillation.

Distillation relies on separating substances with different boiling points by heating them to a critical temperature and condensing the vapour that is given off. Since alcohol has a lower boiling point than water, a heated fermented liquid gives off an even more alcoholic vapour that can then be condensed into a more potent liquid.

Brandy is a distillate of wine, which originated, unsurprisingly, in France in the Middle Ages. Today the majority of quality brandy still comes from France, although other countries – notably the Greeks with their Metaxas – have made a sizeable impact on the market with their exported produce.

Whisky and gin, although different in taste, both begin life as fermented grain and come out of the stills as colourless liquids. Whisky is then aged for several years in oak casks to give it colour and flavour, while gin is used young and has extra flavours – predominantly juniper – added to it.

Vodka is as close to pure alcohol as is physically drinkable. Distilled from virtually any fermentable material, vodkas in the east are flavoured while western vodka is specially treated to remove any flavour other than that of ethyl alcohol.

Whichever country you visit, you will find that it has its own peculiar form of distillate. Normandy ferments apple juice into cider, which is then distilled into calvados. In the Middle East, palm sap, dates, grape juice, molasses and cereals are the raw materials of arrack, arak, raki and ouzo. Scandinavia and Germany are famed for schnapps, while in South America the preferred tipple is tequila, based on the fermented juice of the cactus-like agave plant. Rum, meanwhile, is made from the fermented sugar cane juice and molasses found in the Caribbean, while the king of all distillates – depending on who you talk to of course – is brandy.

In terms of PR, the liqueur absinthe hasn't got a great deal going for it. And yet it earns its little section in this book because any discussion of booze culture simply has to include it. There aren't many alcoholic drinks, after all, that have inspired the world's finest artistic talents to peaks of creative genius and yet spent the best part of a century being banned along with opiates, cocaine and cannabis.

Absinthe is an anise-flavoured liqueur distilled with the oil of wormwood, a leafy herb. Wormwood had been used medicinally since the early Middle Ages to exterminate tapeworms in the abdomen, but in the 18th century it was discovered to have hallucinogenic properties akin to hashish when taken in solution. But because it was so unacceptably bitter, it wasn't popular – indeed, the word absinthe is derived from the Greek *absinthion* meaning 'undrinkable' (and, interestingly, the Russian word for absinthe is *chernobyl*).

In the late 19th century, French distiller Henri-Louis Pernod developed a system of delivering the herb and alcohol in a beverage with a flavour resembling liquorice. The drink immediately became *de rigueur* with such Parisian bohemians as Paul Verlaine, Oscar Wilde and Toulouse Lautrec.

While the psychoactive effect of wormwood helped the elite artists to create, the long-term psychological and physiological consequences of absinthe consumption were having a deleterious effect on the general public. Hospitals across Europe were full of absinthe drinkers suffering from renal failure, convulsions, involuntary incontinence, foaming at the mouth, seizures, chest effusion, red urine and kidney congestion. It was also noted that heavy absinthe drinkers had a propensity towards madness and suicide.

In 1910, the drink was banned in most of Europe, and the USA banned it in 1912. Today, it is only available in Spain, Portugal, the Czech Republic and, surprisingly, the UK where it has never been banned. However, the drink is making a comeback even in countries where it is still illegal. For example, in February 2002, La Fée Verte, a brand of absinthe, was launched in France. The manufacturers managed to sneak it through the net because there is only an oblique reference to absinthe on the label (*la fée verte* means 'green fairy', the old nickname for absinthe) but mainly because its strength is just half of the 70 per cent proof of traditional absinthe.

THE DEMON DRINK – WHAT TOO MUCH DRINK CAN DO TO YOU.
Alcohol provides the 'spirit' to a drink, the mystical warmth that can lift the soul from its darkest recesses. But it is also a poison, and it doesn't take a brain surgeon to deduce that overdosing on alcohol is going to do you no good in the long term. It's estimated that drinking a bottle and a half of spirits or its equivalent at any one time would be enough to kill the average person.

The recommended 'safe' amount to drink, as directed by the World Health Organization, is measured in the now-legendary 'unit'. A unit is the equivalent of one small glass of wine, one 25ml measure of spirits or a half pint of ordinary strength beer or lager. Adult women are recommended to drink no more than two or three units per day, while the limit for men is set at three or four units per day. However, it is estimated that 14 per cent of both sexes regularly consume double this amount. The effects on the body of such overindulgence on a regular basis make for understandably grim reading, according to medical experts.

'Alcohol, in extreme quantities, is like any other lethal chemical,' says French alcohol specialist Dr Patrice Colmiere. 'Over a period of years, constant heavy drinking is going to have a deleterious effect on the internal organs that process alcohol from the system. A glass of wine at meal times is fine, but several bottles a day is going to kill you eventually.'

Here are some of the areas of the body that heavy drinking will affect:

■ **Mental Health** – Alcohol depresses the central nervous system, which is why, in the short term, it reduces inhibitions and tensions. But heavy drinking interferes with the balance of chemicals in the brain. For example, it lowers the production of serotonin, which regulates moods – this leads to mild symptoms of depression, including insomnia, sluggishness, anxiety and loss of concentration.

■ **Weight** – Alcohol is rich in calories. Dry white wine has 85 calories, sweet white wine 120, beer 170 and strong lager as many as 400. Every 3,500 calories consumed over the calorie intake required leads to a $1/2$ kg (1lb) weight gain.

■ **Skin** – Because women's skin is thinner than men's, the effect of drinking on a woman's complexion is more marked. Alcohol dilates blood capillaries, which can cause the face to flush while drinking. The skin also becomes greasy and blemished. Alcohol dries the scalp, too, which leads to severe dandruff and hair loss. The face can become puffy and bloated because alcohol acts as a diuretic, forcing water to leave the body in the form of urine. This stresses the kidneys, causing imbalances in the body's salts, which in turn upset the balance of fluid in the cells, particularly the face.

■ **Pancreas** – Inflammation of the pancreas, known as pancreatitis, can occur in as little as a month of heavy drinking, depending on a person's genetic make up. A woman's pancreas is 50 per cent more vulnerable to alcohol damage than a man's. Symptoms include severe pain in the upper abdomen, while chronic pancreatitis can cause permanent damage to the pancreas and result in it having to be removed.

■ **Kidneys** – Prolonged drinking can cause kidney problems or even renal failure.

■ **Liver** – It is in the liver that the burning-up process of removing alcohol from the body takes place – which is why liver damage is one of the tell-tale signs of the physiological damage being exacted on the body by alcohol. The enzyme within the liver that breaks down alcohol is called alcohol dehydrogenase (ADH). Unfortunately, there isn't a great deal of it about – and certainly not enough to deal comfortably with excessive drinking. Even at full tilt, ADH can only break down and remove alcohol from the blood at a rate of 8g, or one 'unit', an hour. Drinking excessively will therefore, after a while, mean that you can drink more without feeling drunk. But this increased staying power comes at a price: the liver learns to break down alcohol at a faster rate, so more drinks are needed to achieve the same alcohol level in the blood. This activity upsets the liver's enzyme balance, causing it to swell with fatty globules. As alcohol is broken down, it produces a toxic chemical called acetaldehyde, which attacks the liver. The next stage of damage is swelling or hepatitis of the liver. If drinking persists on a damaged liver it can lead to cirrhosis, or scarring, of the liver and eventual death.

According to Chris Day, professor of liver medicine at the University of Newcastle-upon-Tyne, chronic alcohol excess remains the commonest cause of liver disease within hospitals in the UK. 'A typical Regional Liver Unit would expect to see around 500 patients a year with alcoholic liver disease of varying severity. In an audit of all patients admitted to hospitals in Newcastle in 1998 with any form of liver disease, alcohol excess accounted for 38 per cent of patients and, together with hepatitis C, alcoholic liver disease is now the commonest indication for liver transplantation in the UK. Of particular concern is circumstantial evidence that the prevalence of alcoholic liver disease may be increasing in the UK. Death rates from cirrhosis have increased over the past 10 years in both men and women.'

■ **Heart** – High alcohol intake increases levels of cholesterol, which can fur the arteries and lead to heart attacks and strokes.

■ **Fertility** – Even a low consumption of alcohol, such as ten glasses a week, can make it harder for a woman to conceive. This is because alcohol may disrupt the ability of a fertilized egg to implant in the womb. Just a few months of heavy drinking can cause heavy, irregular periods, which also lowers the chances of ovulation. For men, long-term excessive drinking depresses the sperm count. According to a recent survey of persistent heavy drinkers by Australian fertility researchers, 'feminization' occurs – breasts develop and the testicles shrivel as the liver produces globulin, which destroys sex hormones.

■ **Brain** – Specific parts of the brain, most notably the superior frontal cortex, are often damaged in alcoholics. Some research suggests that extended alcohol abuse can result in brain shrinkage. A recent survey, by Dr Duncan Clark of the Pittsburgh Adolescent Alcohol Research Center, revealed that teenagers who drank had smaller hippocampi (the region of the brain associated with memory and learning) than those who didn't. 'The difference between drinkers and non-drinkers is fairly substantial, about a ten per cent difference, which for this region of the brain is a major difference,' said Dr Clark.

While the effect of alcohol on the vital organs is a documented medical fact, the psychological effect is a more complex and debatable matter.

Alcohol, like cannabis, cocaine and any other drug, is a mind-altering substance. 'It stimulates us,' says Jancis Robinson. 'It makes us feel better able to cope with specific problems and with social life in general. It broadens the horizons of possibility and gives us the impression we can achieve more than we can without it.' This is certainly true. Pay a visit to any theme bar on a Friday night and you will see ample evidence of how alcohol perks up the libido, reduces the inhibitions and encourages sex-starved young men to belive that they can achieve more than they can without it. But step outside and witness the hopeless wino in the

> In Germany 2.7 million people between 19 and 69 misuse alcohol. Alcohol-related mortality is currently estimated at over 40,000 a year, whilst in Hungary cirrhosis among the male population rose from 19 per 100,000 in 1970 to 208.8 in 1994.

alleyway, and are you still convinced that alcohol makes us all 'feel better able to cope with specific problems and with social life in general'?

There is no definitive answer to this. Some people can drink and enjoy alcohol all their lives without becoming drunks, in the same way that others can puff away on cannabis joints without becoming heroin addicts. It depends almost entirely on an individual's personality and, more specifically, the personality that lurks behind their inhibitions.

'There was a guy I used to work with,' says financial advisor Mark Sherwen, 29, 'who really was the quietest, least offensive bloke you could ever wish to meet. He'd sit at his desk and hardly say a word. But every time we'd go out on a works piss-up, the guy was a legend. He'd get four or five sherbets down his neck and the next thing you know he's up on the table dropping his trousers and waving his dick around. He'd always get kicked out of the bar, it was hilarious. Next morning, he wouldn't remember a thing.'

Bank clerk Karen Paice, 25, says, 'My old flat mate Briony was a bloody liability when we used to go out. All it took was a couple of glasses of wine and she'd transform into this man-eater. You'd see her disappearing out of the bar on some guy's arm, and the next time you'd see her would be the next morning when she turned up back at the flat looking like she'd been dragged through a hedge backwards. She'd keep saying it wouldn't happen again, but it always did whenever she had a drink.'

And this, from 34-year-old electrician Mike Dampier, 'I don't drink anymore. I don't trust myself. I wasn't an alcoholic or anything, but when I was in my 20s I used to go out at weekends with my mates and just lash into the lager. Eight or nine pints at least. I used to get really shirty with drink. I'd start picking fights with people about nothing. The night wouldn't be complete unless I'd had a rumble. The worst thing was, I thought I was being really cool. I thought all my mates thought I was God's gift. But it was only when one of them told me I was being a total prick that I realized what I was really like.'

These are just three examples of how alcohol can change a personality – or, rather, how alcohol can reveal the personality that we usually keep suppressed. Alcohol may stimulate us but it is, in fact, a depressant more akin to barbiturates and anaesthetic. As we've seen, it reduces the activity of the central nervous system and, in particular, the workings of the brain. The stimulation, even euphoria, we feel after that first glass of wine or tot of whisky is caused by the fact that the mechanisms that usually control our inhibitions have been suppressed. Most startling of all, it can reveal that the apparent introvert is really an extrovert.

'True introverts seem to be comparatively resistant to the effects of alcohol,' said Dr Michael Gossop of the Maudsley Hospital's Drug Dependency Clinical Research and Treatment Unit, 'whereas extroverts succumb to its intoxicating influence more readily. At most parties, the extroverted behaviour of guests can be directly linked to the amount of drink that has been consumed. Drunkenness is a chemical equivalent of extreme extroversion.'

YOU KNOW YOU WANT IT – ALCOHOL AND SEX

MACDUFF: What three things does drink especially promote?

PORTER: Marry sir, nose-painting, sleep, and urine. Lechery, sir it provokes, and unprovokes; it provokes the desire, but it takes away the performance... - From *Macbeth*, Act II, Scene II

Shakespeare's oft-quoted opinion on the effect of alcohol on sexual performance may be correct on a strictly medical basis, but the evidence shows that it doesn't stop people trying – especially young people.

A recent study of American students revealed that as many as 70 per cent of them admit to having engaged in sexual activity primarily as a result of being under the influence of alcohol, while, frighteningly, 90 per cent of all campus rapes occur when alcohol has been used by either the assailant or the victim.

'I was at a party at a friend's apartment right before Thanksgiving break,' said one female student interviewed as part of the survey. 'I got pretty tanked up playing drinking games and suddenly I was outside on this fire escape with a guy I'd met an hour earlier. I was doing something to him I'd rather not talk about. The next morning I woke up and couldn't even remember his name. I felt disgusted. To make matters worse, either someone saw us or he bragged to his friends about what happened, because after I got back from the break a friend of mine told me I had a new nickname.'

And it's not just women who wake up feeling used and abused after a night on the sauce, as this cautionary tale from the same survey reveals: 'One Thursday night I was out with my friends, kicking off the weekend. This girl challenged me to a drinking contest, so I took her up on it and we got really drunk. She came back to my room after last call. We hung out, drank a few more beers, and I guess I passed out. I don't know how much time had passed, but I woke up to her on top of me. Apparently my body was in the mood to have sex, even though I wasn't mentally interested at all. She had already gotten going before I managed to push her off me. There was no protection involved. I know it's hard to believe that a guy can be raped, but I really felt violated. I did not want to have sex with her. To make things worse, about a month later I realized I'd contracted herpes.'

Over recent years, research into the phenomenon of alcohol and teenage sex have produced more sobering facts. One study of girls aged 14-21 experiencing unplanned pregnancies found that a third of them were drinking when they had sex, and that 90 per cent hadn't even planned to have sex. Similarly, the more teenagers drink the less they use condoms. Teenagers who had five or more drinks were three times less likely to use condoms than other teenagers.

How does this square with the perceived wisdom that drinking heavily stops you 'getting it up'? Shakespeare was quite correct. Blood alcohol levels starting at as little as 30mg per 100ml pharmacologically decrease inhibitions, which can enhance sexual arousal. But once levels reach over 100mg, everything changes. In men, erection and ejaculatory competence are inhibited or eliminated. In women too much alcohol can result in lack of orgasms, painful intercourse and low arousal. In the long term, a whole host of horrors can be visited on the male drinker including atrophy of the testicles and the destruction of the male sex hormone.

The problem for both sexes would appear to be the period when the blood alcohol level is between 30mg and the cut-off point of 100mg. This is when arousal is at its highest and inhibitions at their lowest. However, in order to speed things up, an entirely more sinister method of encouraging sex has become widespread, in which drugs are insinuated into alcoholic drink.

In the 1960s, young people occasionally popped sedatives such as Quaaludes to loosen their inhibitions. These were commonly known as 'love drugs' and were relatively harmless. The drug that has hit the headlines in recent years, however, is Rohypnol, and an indication of its effect is that it is more commonly known as 'the date-rape drug'.

Rohypnol – otherwise known as 'roofies', 'ruffies', 'roche', 'R-2', 'rib' and 'rope' – is a brand name for flunitrazepam, a very potent tranquillizer similar in nature to Valium but about ten times stronger. The drug, manufactured and distributed worldwide by the Hoffman-LaRoche company, produces a sedative effect, amnesia, muscle relaxation and a slowing of psychomotor responses. The effects last for several hours. Although it is not commonly used by doctors, and in the USA is not even listed in the pharmacopoeia, the drug is often distributed on the street in its original bubblewrap, which adds an air of legitimacy.

Illicit use of Rohypnol was first reported in Europe in the late 1970s, and its use has spread exponentially since then. In the US, 'roofies' were first seen in the early 1990s, where they quickly became popular among high school and college students, as well as among the gay community. The drug is often combined with marijuana and cocaine to produce a dramatic high – but it is at its most effective when added to alcohol, which can often occur without the drinker knowing about it. On most occasions the first time a victim knows she/he has been date raped is when she/he wakes up with no clothes on in a strange flat.

The message from police is to increase vigilance and never take your eyes off your drink. In some university bars, campaigners leave little flags in unattended drinks, saying, 'This could have been a date-rape drug.' In Oxfordshire, following a spate of date rapes, scientists even developed a hi-tech cocktail stirrer that can detect the presence of certain drugs and then changes colour to alert the drinker.

ON THE LASH – BINGE DRINKING

Duncan Brydewell didn't have a drink problem. The 34-year-old from North London rarely ventured into pubs during the week, and he preferred a cup of tea in the evening to a glass of whisky or wine. In fact, the only time Duncan liked a drink was on a Saturday. He would go to the pub at opening time, resplendent in his Tottenham Hotspur replica football shirt, and wolf down nine or ten lagers before heading off to the match with his mates. Afterwards he would go straight back to the pub, where a couple of post-match swifties would be the prelude to a crawl around six or seven local bars, where he had been known to consume as many as 20 pints, not to mention the odd alcopop here and there for variation. Duncan was never any bother; he could hold his drink. But one day, shortly after his 34th birthday, Duncan began to feel unwell. He went to the doctor, who took some tests and diagnosed cirrhosis of the liver. Duncan was horrified. Cirrhosis was the kind of thing other people got, winos who drank neat meths 24 hours of every day. There had to be some mistake. There was not. Six months later, Duncan was dead.

It's a sad tale, but one that is becoming increasingly common as the so-called 'binge-drinking culture' is adopted by more and more young people. In December 2001, the UK's Chief Medical Officer released a report that showed that, while liver cirrhosis deaths have risen in most age groups over the last 30 years, the increase among people aged 35–44 is especially worrying. There has been an eight-fold rise in deaths among men and a six-fold increase among women of this age group. Even among 25-34-year-olds there has been a three-fold rise in the death toll over the last 30 years.

Death from alcohol-related liver disease among binge drinkers (classified in certain instances as people who drink more than five drinks in a row), is not only confined to the UK. According to the World Health Organization (WHO), bingeing is becoming an epidemic right across Europe. As many as one in eight deaths among young men in western Europe are related to drink. In former Eastern Bloc countries such as Russia, the Ukraine, Hungary, Lithuania, and Estonia, the drink-related toll is one-in-three male, and one-in-eight female, deaths.

Alcohol poisoning is the most serious immediate consequence of binge drinking. When excessive amounts of alcohol are consumed, the brain is deprived of oxygen. The struggle to deal with an overdose of alcohol coupled with a lack of oxygen will eventually cause the brain to shut down the voluntary functions that regulate breathing and heart rate.

'We are receiving signals from all across Europe that many young people are turning to alcohol as a drug,' said Cees Goos, WHO regional advisor for alcohol, drugs and tobacco. 'There is an increase in high-risk drinking, such as binge-drinking and drunkenness.'

The WHO report highlighted the drinking profile of many individual countries within Europe.

- **Belgium** – Six per cent of workers have drink problems; 40 per cent of violent crime and vandalism is linked to alcohol.
- **Denmark** – Drink-related deaths doubled between 1970–94 despite national consumption having stagnated since 1983.

- **Finland** - Nearly half of male and one-in-five female suicides involve alcohol abusers.
- **France** - 40 per cent of fatal traffic accidents - 4,000 deaths a year - and overall 43,000 deaths, 9 per cent of the total deaths that year, were linked to drink in 1997.
- **Germany** - 2.7 million people between the ages of 9 and 69 misuse alcohol. Alcohol-related mortality is estimated at 40,000 a year.
- **Hungary** - Cirrhosis among men rose from 19 per 100,000 in 1970 to 208.8 in 1994.
- **Norway** - 80 per cent of crimes of violence and 60 per cent of rapes, arson and vandalism are committed under the influence.
- **Poland** - There were 1,446 fatal alcohol poisonings in 1996.
- **Russia** - 40 per cent of men and 17 per cent of women suffer from alcoholism.
- **Spain** - 25 per cent of all domestic violence is drink-related.
- **Sweden** - In 1992, 87 per cent of attempted suicides were attributable to alcohol.
- **United Kingdom** - 50 per cent of violent crime and 65 per cent of attempted suicides are due to alcohol. In England and Wales alone, 33,000 deaths a year can be linked to drink.

Across the Atlantic, the same problem has reared its head in America. Recent reports suggest that college students - most of whom are officially barred from drinking by laws that fix the minimum age for buying at 21 - are killing themselves at a rate of 1,400 a year in drink-related incidents. According to researchers at Boston University, alcohol also contributes to an estimated 500,000 student injuries and 70,000 cases of sexual assault.

As with the rest of the world, it is binge drinking that is the root of the problem in the US. The research indicates that more than 40 per cent of students binge drink. 'Students here don't tend to drink very often, but when they do they drink a lot,' 21-year-old Harvard student Joe Flood said. 'They don't learn how to drink sensibly. You've either got to have a 21-year-old in the group or a fake ID. So it's more someone sneaking a bottle of vodka into their rooms and drinking it all.'

DROWNING IN DRINK? – THE ALCOHOL EPIDEMIC

If we take the statistics at face value, alcohol is running riot throughout the world like an outbreak of the plague. According to one piece of conservative research, alcohol abuse costs every country the equivalent of £3 billion ($4.42 billion) every year in medical treatment – more than any other accident or illness. Even the so-called 'sophisticated' drinkers of France and Italy seem to pay a terrible price for their enjoyment of alcohol: in Italy, 22 out of every 100,000 people die each year from chronic liver disease, compared to 16 per 100,000 in wine-loving France. This is nothing compared to the 28 per 100,000 who regularly drink themselves into an early grave in the Ukraine, while figures for the rest of the former Soviet Union states, while not definitively recorded, are thought to be even higher.

In the USA, more than 35,000 people died of cirrhosis of the liver alone in 1995, while there were an estimated 7 million alcohol abusers and 11 million alcoholics. 'The USA is a big country,' said one US health expert, 'but these figures are just crazy. You're talking about the numerical equivalent of an entire state whose lives have been ruined by alcohol.'

In the UK, there are more than 28,000 hospital admissions each year caused by alcohol dependence or poisoning. Such is the weight of alcohol-related problems that many believe the health service is about to crack under the strain. 'The NHS is on the brink of collapse and health professionals are on the brink of despair,' says Dr Chris Luke of Cork University Hospital. 'If one issue illustrates why there is this despair it is the issue of alcohol. Alcohol is a lifestyle issue which grows with affluence and is continuing to worsen steadily.'

Although it would be fatuous to suggest that drinking levels are anything like as bad as they were during the gin-swilling 1700s, increasing numbers of experts are beginning to use the word 'epidemic' when it comes to alcohol consumption in 21st-century Britain. In 2001, Alcohol Concern revealed that 1 person in every 13 is dependent on alcohol in Britain – twice as many as are hooked on all forms of drugs, including prescription drugs. Estimates of the total number of deaths where alcohol has played a part range up to 33,000 every year. The survey went on to say that, after a night on the pop, one in four people say they have experienced memory loss, injured themselves or another or failed to do what is expected of them – like turn up for work.

'The sheer breadth and scale of the problems – in terms of their impact on people's health, relationships and pockets, not to mention on public services, especially the NHS – reinforces the need for urgent joined-up action at a national level,' said Eric Appleby, director of Alcohol Concern.

Another concern is the steady global increase in drinking in the workplace. In the UK 8-14 million working days are lost each year through drink-related absenteeism, with a cost to industry estimated at over £600 million ($883.3 million) in England and Wales alone. In the US, the cost is estimated at $75–100 billion (£51-67.9 billion). Drinkers take four times as many days off as other employees, and one in five industrial accidents are alcohol related. Add to this the lateness due to hangovers, long lunch hours, impaired decision-making, reduced reaction times and efficiency in the afternoon, and a poor image presented to customers, and it's no surprise that employers are increasingly cracking down on drinking during working hours.

Drinking in the workplace is a worldwide concern. The International Labour Organization estimates that globally 3–5 per cent of the average workforce are alcohol dependent, and up to 25 per cent drink heavily enough to be at risk of dependence.

In the US, alcohol is the most widely abused drug among working adults. An estimated 6.2 per cent of adults working full time are heavy drinkers, while up to 40 per cent of industrial fatalities and 47 per cent

> In England and Wales, 33,000 people a year are dying from drink-induced causes, including ill health, road crashes, violence, alcohol poisoning and other accidents.

of industrial injuries can be linked to alcohol consumption and alcoholism. A stark example of what can happen when alcohol affects the workplace is the 1989 Exxon Valdez disaster, in which the drunken crew allowed the tanker to founder off the coast of Alaska, causing widespread ecological damage. The reaction has been strict workplace clampdowns, with instant dismissal a common punishment, and some companies going so far as to breathalyze employees in key positions. Some firms – especially safety-conscious oil and transport firms and Anglo-US companies – have already implemented random breathalyzer tests for their employees. However, in general, Europe takes a more laid-back view of drinking. In Belgium, for example, a recent study showed that over 60 per cent of companies did not have any formal procedures on alcohol abuse in the workplace. Similar studies in France, Portugal and Greece found limited official corporate policies on the abuse of alcohol among workers.

MAKE MINE A BABYCHAM...AND FOUR LAGERS – WOMEN DRINKERS

Described as an 'everyday drinker' by a fashionable UK women's magazine, 40-year-old knitwear designer Berni Yates described her weekly drinking habits in diary form for one of its journalists:

WEEK 1
- **Monday** – Small bottle of lager, spritzer, 1.5 bottles of white wine.
- **Tuesday, Wednesday And Thursday** – One lager, one bottle of white wine each day.
- **Friday** – Two lagers, three glasses of wine, three vodka-Red Bulls, seven spritzers.
- **Saturday** – Two beers, one bottle of wine.
- **Sunday** – Two beers, 1.5 bottles of wine.

WEEK 2
- **Monday** – Two beers, one bottle of wine.
- **Tuesday** – One beer, 1.5 bottles of wine.
- **Wednesday** – Two glasses of wine, plus one bottle at home.
- **Thursday** – One bottle of wine.
- **Friday** – Two beers, four glasses of wine, four bottles of K.
- **Saturday** – Two glasses of wine, plus two bottles of wine.
- **Sunday** – Half a bottle of wine.

'Alcohol seems to be an accompaniment to much of Berni's domestic routine,' said the magazine's expert. 'She is, I think, psychologically dependent on alcohol. A maximum of 21 units per week is a safe level. At

35 units or more you really should look at changing your drinking behaviour. Berni averaged 75 units a week.'

If there is any consolation for Berni, it is that she does not drink alone. According to the Medical Council on Alcohol, there has been a dramatic increase in excessive drinking among women – and especially women aged between 18 and 40. In a recent study by Edinburgh City Hospital's Alcohol and Health Research Centre, 85 per cent of women said they consumed alcohol, compared to 91 per cent of men. Meanwhile a government report revealed the sobering statistic that cirrhosis of the liver now kills more women than cervical cancer does. Most amazing of all, perhaps, is the survey that shows more women than men are participating in the 3,400 Alcoholics Anonymous groups in the UK.

Times have changed since Hollywood studio heads, shocked by Greta Garbo swilling whisky in the 1930 film *Anna Christie*, enforced the Hay Code, which forbade the portrayal of sex between unmarried couples and insisted that only men drank alcohol on screen. The writer Christina Odone notes that it is 'incredible to think that only a few decades on, a woman of [TV presenter] Anne Robinson's status would publish a grisly memoir of her alcohol-induced self-destruction, replete with harrowing vignettes of waking up in a pool of her own vomit in a strange bed and staggering off to the off-licence at 9am to buy her first miniature bottle. That the megastar should dare flaunt her cautionary tale signals a recognition that there are thousands of women out there for whom a drink means everything.'

Pressure to keep up with macho workplace culture, and heavy advertising of female-oriented bottled cocktails and sweeter drinks, have been blamed. Movies like *Bridget Jones's Diary*, it seems, accurately portray the current vogue for uncontrolled bingeing followed by guilty abstinence. Richard Robinson, of market analyst Datamonitor, said, 'Many women follow a "debits" and "credits" system which sees them feeling that one session of "being good", such as going to the gym, earns them an indulgence such as an alcoholic drink. Consumers feel more comfortable about their alcohol intake as they feel able to justify it to themselves.'

In terms of what women drink, the days of sweet white wine are long gone. More and more women now increasingly turn to premium bottled lagers and pre-mixed spirits. As we have seen, the deliberate conversion of bars and pubs from predominantly male bastions into unisex areas has seen a marked increase in the number of women drinkers (see p39). In terms of units of alcohol consumed, British women (9.4 units) still lag behind their counterparts in France, Germany, Italy and Spain. But by 2004, consumption is expected to be 11.8 units – behind only Germany on 14.3 and France on 12.9.

A familiar story emanates from the USA, where the *Journal Of American College Health* reports that between 1993 and 2001 all-women colleges saw an increase of 125 per cent in frequent binge drinking – accompanied by a 150 per cent rise in 'unplanned sexual activity'. In middle-class sorority houses, young women are drinking ferociously and, typically, twice as many girls as boys are being treated for chronic intoxication. At the elite Georgetown University in Washington DC, there has been a 35 per cent rise in the number of women sanctioned for alcohol violations in the past three years. Dessa Bergen Cico, the Dean of students at Syracuse University said, 'Women are drinking one for one with men, but they are coming in much more damaged.'

Meanwhile, in the ghettos of major US cities, social workers are reporting that alcohol is now more of a threat to young women than drugs are. Chicago Baptist minister Rev Dan Taylor says, 'Girls are coming for counselling having had their stomachs pumped in hospitals, others with fractured bones after drunken fights, some who have been sexually assaulted while they were incapable of resistance.'

Posters currently appearing in student bars across the USA sum up the pitfalls of boozing for their women customers, 'If you're drunk you'll have sex with someone you wouldn't have lunch with.'

Cirrhosis and sexually transmitted diseases are not the only potential health nightmares for women who drink to excess. The increasing number of women drinkers has coincided with a whole raft of medical research into the effects of alcohol on the female body. Much of it makes grim reading for Bridget Jones enthusiasts.

One scare story concerns the possible correlation between drinking and the incidence of breast cancer. In 1987, the results of research projects at Harvard Medical School and the US National Cancer Institute at Bethesda, Maryland revealed that women who drank between three and nine drinks

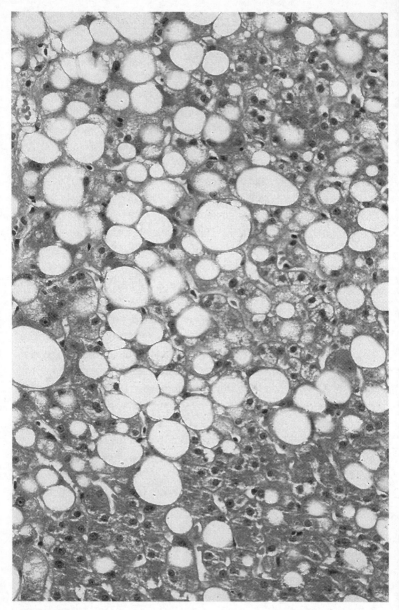

Light micrograph of a section through the liver of an alcoholic, showing fat droplets distending the liver cells. The fat was destroyed in the preparation of the slide, leaving unstained areas of vacuoles (white circles). This condition occurs in most heavy drinkers from time to time and is caused by continually high levels of alcohol in the blood disturbing the normal process of metabolising fat. Fatty deposits in the liver can also be caused by hypoxia, toxins, or diabetes mellitus.

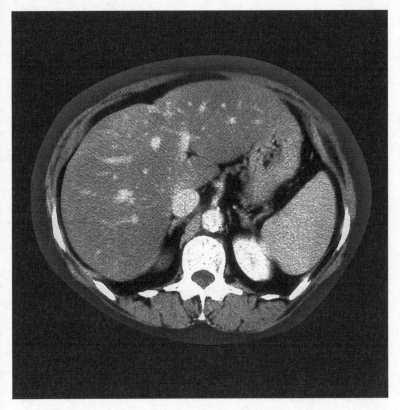

CT (Computed Tomography) scan of an axial section through the abdomen of a 66-year-old woman suffering from fatty liver. The white shape (LOWER CENTRE) is a bone of the vertebra. The liver is the large organ occupying much of the abdomen (UPPER LEFT-RIGHT). The liver cells have become swollen by large droplets of fat.

a week were 30 per cent more likely to develop breast cancer than non-drinkers, while those who drank more than nine drinks a week increased their risk of breast cancer by 60 per cent.

Another area of major research is alcohol and pregnancy. In 1973, a generation of women were introduced to Foetal Alcohol Syndrome (FAS) thanks to three American researchers who identified physiological and mental similarities between eight children born to chronically alcoholic mothers who continued to drink during their pregnancies. Abnormalities in these children included general developmental delay, mental retardation, hyperactivity and short attention spans, as well as physiological traits such as small, upturned noses, receding foreheads and chins, sunken nasal bridges and abnormal ears.

As most newborn babies exhibit some or all of these characteristics in the first weeks of their lives, FAS sent women into paroxysms of terror – until it was pointed out that the mothers of children identified with the syndrome were serious alcohol abusers from underprivileged backgrounds who also partook in tobacco and illicit drugs to excess. 'In general, women who drink heavily also smoke heavily and frequently use other drugs,' said Dr Moira Plant, of the Alcohol Research Group in Edinburgh. 'Their diet is often poor and their general lifestyles unhealthy. It may be this whole lifestyle which determines the risk to the foetus and not one single factor.'

Perhaps one of the most important things for the modern, liberated, beer-swilling babe to understand is that, while their careers and pub-going are now on a par with men's, women's bodies are unfortunately not when it comes to alcohol. Women have more fat and less fluid than men's, so even if they are a similar size and weight and drink the same amount, the concentration of alcohol in their blood will be higher. Women are also more sensitive to the immediate effects of drinking during ovulation and in the two or three days before a period. They are likely to feel the effects of alcohol more quickly at these times than they would normally.

The best way to keep up with men at the bar, according to US researchers, is to stick to beer. A team from Mount Sinai School of Medicine in New York measured the activity of three stomach enzymes that work on breaking down alcohol, and found that men's are twice as effective as women's. This did not seem to matter so much when beer of 5 per cent alcohol was being served, but when concentrations got to 10 per cent, or 40 per cent for scotch or vodka, the difference showed.

'In other words, women respond to beer in the same way as men, but not to wine or hard spirits,' said researcher Charles Leiber. 'In general, both women and female animals are more susceptible to the negative or toxic effects of alcohol. This is true for the liver, heart muscle, skeletal muscle, and it may be true for the pancreas and the brain.'

THE LOST WEEKEND AND BEYOND – ALCOHOLISM

The late Dylan Thomas wrote, 'An alcoholic is someone you don't like who drinks as much as you,' and as a legendary alcoholic himself, he should have known what he was talking about. We have already discussed how alcoholics, alcohol dependants or alcohol addicts – the semantics are up to you – are regarded in a sympathetic way while heroin addicts, for example, are despised. Perhaps this is because 85 per cent of the world's population drinks alcohol, compared to the less than one per cent that takes heroin. But perhaps it is because alcoholism is such a deceptively easy state into which to fall that we all find ourselves uttering the mantra 'there but for the grace of God go I' whenever we see someone who has become dependent on the demon drink.

Unlike tobacco, cocaine or heroin, dependency on alcohol tends not to be measured in terms of the quantity consumed, but rather in the degree of compulsion. A number of danger signals have been identified that may indicate the slippery slope towards full-blown alcoholism.

■ The compulsion to drink at certain times of the day.
   'When I get home I find I am so wound up by the kids and by the job that I simply cannot unwind without a glass or two of wine.'
   – Jane, 42, teacher

■ Emotional upset when a drink is denied.
   'It's not as if I need a drink – but I don't like to be told I can't have one if I want one. That really gets on my nerves.' – Pete, 34, travel agent

■ The manipulation of routine and habits to suit, enable or favour drinking activity.

'I started coming up with this cock-and-bull stuff about how a Sunday lunchtime pint was part of a great heritage that should never be allowed to die. In reality, I just wanted to get some beers down my neck to top up from Saturday night.' - Daniel, 29, journalist

■ Raising drinking to an activity with a higher priority than commitments to family and friends.

'The lure of the pub - what can you say? There was one occasion when Jean and I had invited the whole family round for supper. I was just leaving work when one of the lads suggested a swift pint. Five hours later I staggered in, totally hammered. It took Jean about a month to speak to me again.'

- Gareth, 31, computer programmer

■ Difficulty controlling the amount drunk.

'I know you're supposed to stick to weekly units, but it's like sticking to a diet. Impossible. I'll go out with all the best intentions in the world, but I can't help getting carried away and necking three or four times more than I should.' - Katie, 23, student

■ The emergence of a daily drinking routine.

'My grandfather always went out at 9pm, on the dot, and had four pints down the pub with his mates. My dad did the same, and now I do, too. It's got to the stage when I start to get fidgety at quarter to nine.' - David, 33, line manager

■ Altered tolerance to alcohol.

'When I was in my 20s, I could have drunk for England. Eight or nine pints, no bother at all. You would never have known I'd had a drink. Not any more. I have a couple and I'm starting to feel a bit tanked. I think if I had eight or nine, I'd be on my back.'

- Paul, 36, actor

- Physical withdrawal symptoms upon abstention.
  'It used to be a standing joke – waking up the morning after with shaking hands and cold sweat. But I got the shock of my life when my hands started shaking and I started getting the jitters when I went a couple of days without a drink. "My God!" I thought, "I'm turning into a wino."' - Lesley, 38, council liaison officer

- Drinking to avoid withdrawal symptoms.
  'The day I realized I had a problem was the day I found myself pouring a slug of Macallan into my morning cuppa, just to stop me feeling like shit from the night before.' - Graeme, 40, police officer

One of the main examples of how our view of alcohol addiction differs from that of other drug addiction is the way that alcoholics are described as victims of a disease. In the 1980s, this was perfectly illustrated when the Alcohol Clinics in the UK changed their name to Alcohol Problem Centres. Some 60 years earlier, Alcoholics Anonymous was set up in the USA on the very premise that certain people are mentally, physically and even chemically susceptible to the Dark Side.

Why then do some drinkers develop alcohol dependence while others do not? One theory is that drinking problems tend to run in families – the children of heavy drinkers are at greater risk of later having trouble with their drinking than are those of parents for whom drinking has never been a problem. In 1992, a study of 23,000 American drinkers seemed to back this up when it revealed that the odds of developing a drinking problem were increased by 86 per cent for people who had a parent or sibling with such a problem, while having both a close and a more distant relative put up the odds by 167 per cent.

So are you doomed if your dad liked his drink? Griffith Edwards (Emeritus Professor of Addiction at the University of London) argues that the theory is simplistic to say the least: 'All right, alcoholism runs in families. But in many cultures so does being a tinker, tailor, soldier or sailor. Children follow in their parents' footsteps mostly because of role modelling and opportunity, not because of genetics. Perhaps drinking runs in families not because of anything written into people's genes but because of home influences.'

Perhaps unsurprisingly, the US-based National Association for Children of Alcoholics (NACA) believes both arguments are true. According to their research, around 76 million Americans – 43 per cent of the adult population – have been exposed to alcoholism in the family, with almost one in five living with an alcoholic while growing up. At any one time NACA claim there are over 26 million children of alcoholics in the US, with over 11 million under the age of 18. Ominously, they point out, 'Children living with a non-recovering alcoholic score lower on measures of family cohesion, intellectual-cultural orientation, active-recreational orientation, and independence. They also usually experience higher levels of conflict within the family'.

> The French call a hangover 'wood mouth', Germans refer to it as 'wailing of the cats', Italians call it 'out of tune', Norwegians identify it as 'carpenters in the head', Spaniards call it 'backlash', and Swedes refer to it as 'pain in the hair roots'.

In the UK, the pressure group Alcohol Concern has conducted its own research into an estimated 920,000 children whose parents are heavy drinkers. It claims that young children in families with a drinking parent have rates of psychiatric disorder at the age of 15 between 2.2 to 3.9 times higher than other young people. 'Celebrating major events like birthdays often becomes impossible,' says Alcohol Concern. 'Coming home from school can be frightening because children will never know what they may find. Many have seen their parent unconscious, injured and bleeding, vomiting or incontinent and have had to deal with these situations. Often children feel guilty and to blame, believing that if they were better behaved or more successful their parent would have no need to drink. Some children become difficult and unruly, some withdraw into themselves. Virtually all children whose parents have an alcohol problem feel lonely and 'switched off', both from relationships within their family and with other people, in particular because families often work very hard to keep problem drinking a secret from the rest of the world.'

'That's bullshit,' says Mark Proudlock, a 27-year-old sports injury therapist from the Midlands. 'My dad was an alcoholic, but he was treated in our family the way you would treat someone with an illness. We rallied round, tried to help him out as best we could. People seem to think that alcoholics are permanently pissed comedy characters, rolling around bumping into furniture. To be honest, you would never have known dad was drunk. It affected his health the same way cancer would. It was a tragedy for him, but it never affected me and my brothers and sisters in the cataclysmically awful way these shrinks seem to assume it does. If anything, it brought us together as a family.'

No matter how a family deals with an alcoholic within its ranks, there is no doubt that the illness has a profound effect not only on the individual, but on those who are close to him or her. Alcoholism can be treated but, as alcoholics themselves admit it, can never fully be cured. The mantra is 'take one day at a time'; but it is all too easy to fall off the precipice.

ARE YOU AN ALCOHOLIC? – THE MAST TEST

When it comes to deciding whether a person has alcohol problems, professionals use a number of tests. The most common is the Michigan Alcohol Screening Test (MAST), which consists of a series of questions that require a simple 'yes' or 'no' answer. The MAST focuses on the consequences of problem drinking and on the subjects' own perceptions of their alcohol problems. It has been widely used in a variety of settings with varied populations. These include alcoholics, persons convicted of driving while intoxicated, other social or problem drinkers, drug abusers, psychiatric patients and general medical patients.

1. Do you feel you are a normal drinker? (By normal, we mean you drink less than or as much as most other people.) [no = 2 points]
2. Have you ever awakened the morning after some drinking the night before and found that you could not remember a part of the evening? [yes = 2 points]
3. Does your wife, husband, a parent or other near relative ever worry or complain about your drinking? [yes = 1 point]
4. Can you stop drinking without a struggle after one or two drinks? [no = 2 points]

5. Do you ever feel guilty about your drinking? [yes = 1 point]
6. Do friends or relatives think you are a normal drinker? [no = 2 points]
7. Are you able to stop drinking when you want to? [no = 2 points]
8. Have you ever attended a meeting of Alcoholics Anonymous (AA)? [yes = 5 points]
9. Have you gotten into physical fights when drinking? [yes = 1 point]
10. Has your drinking ever created a problem between you and your wife, husband, a parent, or other relative? [yes = 2 points]
11. Has your wife, husband, or other family members ever gone to anyone for help about your drinking? [yes = 2 points]
12. Have you ever lost friends because of your drinking? [yes = 2 points]
13. Have you ever gotten into trouble at work or school because of drinking? [yes = 2 points]
14. Have you ever lost a job because of drinking? [yes = 2 points]
15. Have you ever neglected your obligations, your family or your work for two or more days in a row because you were drinking? [yes = 2 points]
16. Do you drink before noon fairly often? [yes: 1 point]
17. Have you ever been told you have liver trouble? Cirrhosis? [yes = 2 points]
18. After heavy drinking have you ever had Delirium Tremens (DTs) or severe shaking, heard voices, or seen things that really weren't there? [yes = 2 points]
19. Have you ever gone to anyone for help about your drinking? [yes = 5 points]
20. Have you ever been in a hospital because of drinking? [yes = 5 points]
21. Have you ever been a patient in a psychiatric hospital or on a psychiatric ward of a general hospital where drinking was part of the problem that resulted in hospitalization? [yes = 2 points]
22. Have you ever been seen at a psychiatric or mental health clinic or gone to any doctor, social worker or clergyman for help with any emotional problem, where drinking was part of the problem? [yes = 2 points]
23. Have you ever been arrested for drunk driving, driving while intoxicated or driving under the influence of alcoholic beverages? [yes = 2 points]

24. Have you ever been arrested, or taken into custody, even for a few hours, because of other drunk behaviour? [yes = 2 points]

Scoring system: In general, five points or more would place the subject in an 'alcoholic' category. Four points would be suggestive of alcoholism, three points or less would indicate the subject was not alcoholic.

TWELVE STEPS TO HEAVEN – ALCOHOLICS ANONYMOUS

We don't know the names of the New York stockbroker and the Ohio surgeon who, in 1935, formed Alcoholics Anonymous. To its 2.2 million members in 134 countries, that is part of the attraction. Names are not important. What is, however, is confronting a drinking habit that has got seriously out of hand, and being able to announce that they are alcoholics in the company of others that have the same problem and will support them.

AA began in the United States just two years after Prohibition ended. Alcohol consumption never really stopped during those dry years – but it's safe to say that once it was given the green light, a lot of people made up for lost time. Interestingly, though, AA's philosophy has always been to blame the alcoholic rather than the alcohol. At no stage have they ever sought to get alcohol banned. The aim of meetings is to encourage members to 'achieve sobriety by staying away from one drink, one day at a time' because those same members have proved that they can't handle drink.

To help them in their quest AA devised its famous Twelve Steps to Recovery, a mantra that members are encouraged not only to follow but adopt as a daily life plan.

THE TWELVE STEPS

1. We admitted we were powerless over alcohol – that our lives had become unmanageable.
2. Came to believe that a Power greater than ourselves could restore us to sanity.
3. Made a decision to turn our will and our lives over to the care of God as we understood Him.

4. Made a searching and fearless moral inventory of ourselves.
5. Admitted to God, and ourselves, and to another human being the exact nature of our wrongs.
6. Were entirely ready to have God remove all these defects of character.
7. Humbly asked Him to remove our shortcomings.
8. Made a list of all persons we had harmed, and became willing to make amends to them all.
9. Made direct amends to such people wherever possible, except when to do so would injure them or others.
10. Continued to take personal inventory and when we were wrong promptly admitted it.
11. Sought through prayer and meditation to improve our conscious contact with God as we understood Him, praying only for knowledge of His will for us and the power to carry that out.
12. Having had a spiritual awakening as the result of these steps, we tried to carry this message to alcoholics, and to practise these principles in all our affairs.

If that all seems somewhat quasi-religious in tone, then it is entirely in keeping with the road-to-Damascus conversion that many recovering AA members claim to experience after quitting the booze. 'I feel like a totally different person,' said one. 'Everywhere I am in the world now, every city, I make a point of seeking out the nearest AA centre and sitting in on meetings. I feel that by sharing my experience I can help others.'

Another said, 'I now have two birthdays every year – the day on which I was born, and the day I accepted I was an alcoholic.'

But does it really work? While AA has undoubtedly helped millions of alcoholics, it is not a sure fire cure to the deep-seated problems that may have started them on the slippery slope. Indeed, it is a fair assumption that almost as many would-be members have left AA meetings and headed straight for the nearest bar.

As Griffith Edwards points out, 'It is not unreasonable conjecture that AA probably works, in some way or other, for not less than 50 per cent of the troubled drinkers who make contact with it. It seems evident that the reason why people sit around in church halls, hospitals, prisons and all manner of other settings to attend AA and talk its talk is because this fellowship meets their needs'.

'A BOTTLE OF WHISKY A DAY' – AN ALCOHOLIC'S STORY

To the moderate, or even heavy drinker, the sheer volume and variety of booze consumed by a true hopeless alcoholic is quite staggering – as is the deleterious effect on the body.

David Beacham (not his real name) is a 31-year-old reformed alcoholic who these days wakes up in the morning with a mixture of gratitude and amazement. A drinker from the age of 12, by the time he was 23 his boozing had led him to incarceration in a mental hospital, at which point he had just weeks to live. 'At university I was drinking a bottle of whisky a day – and that's when I started to get ill,' he recalls. 'I was underweight because I wasn't eating and I was having hallucinations. My gums would always be bleeding and I used to have a pain like acid indigestion which meant I couldn't sleep lying down at night. I had to prop myself up.'

There are an estimated 49 million bubbles in a bottle of champagne. Early wine makers saw such bubbles as a highly undesirable defect to be prevented.

David's drinking history is one that is common in most alcoholics. Aged just 12, he would get his father to buy litre bottles of cider, claiming they were for him and his friends to take to parties. In fact, David was chugging the bottles back himself. By the age of 16, he was a regular in pubs on Friday and Saturday nights, easily able to convince uninterested landlords that he was 18. At home, he would retreat to his bedroom to listen to records and drink cans of beer. By the time he was legally old enough to drink, David was already on the rocky road: 'At 18, I was regularly drinking 12 pints a night and then driving home from the pub. I got caught twice, once aged 20, when I got an 18-month ban and then when I was about a week away from getting my licence back, I got caught again and got a three-year ban.'

The warnings were clearly there, but by now David was stretching beyond the realms of being a heavy drinker to becoming completely alcohol dependent. An intelligent pupil, he easily got the grades required to study politics at Exeter University – and found the drinking culture of student life entirely to his tastes. During his three-year sojourn at Exeter he ran up debts of over £6,000 ($8,833) on booze, filling in the hours when the union bar wasn't open by drinking bottles of spirits. By the time his final year arrived, David was already showing signs of mental deterioration. 'As I got towards my finals, my mental state was such that I was beginning to feel suicidal. I was drinking before exams in the morning.'

Somehow, David managed to scrape a decent enough degree and, despite his alcoholism, was able to secure to a reasonable job with a finance company in London. But the clock was ticking, and it wasn't long before David's monumental consumption began to affect his mind: 'I would have auditory and visual hallucinations and terrible fears that people in my office were the devil. I had delusions that the company I was working for was full of vampires. It was hardly surprising, because I was drinking about 400 units of alcohol a week at the time.'

The end came when David went on a huge drinking spree one day. For some reason he rang his father, who immediately came and took him home. David awoke the next morning with an extreme case of DTs, delirium, hallucinations, and a heart rate going through the roof: 'I was literally climbing up the walls. The ambulance crew wanted to section me, but eventually they agreed to take me to the hospital. The doctors told my dad that if I'd arrived four minutes later I would have had permanent brain damage and if I'd been seven minutes later I would have been dead. I was in accident and emergency, strapped to a trolley. My sister said it looked like a scene from *The Exorcist*.'

His physical condition stabilized, David was transferred to the local mental hospital, where he was diagnosed with alcohol-induced psychosis and sedated with large quantities of medication. Upon his release, he relied upon Diazepam – a drug prescribed to treat anxiety disorders – to try and suppress his drinking. But although he was not drinking as much, David knew that he was treading a thin line: 'Sometimes I felt that I was dying, and if I had another fit I would die in Broadmoor [Prison]. Physically I had no obvious problems, but there were times when I was bleeding and found blood in my underwear. It would terrify me, but I wouldn't see a doctor. I would be aware my kidneys were aching like crazy when I wasn't drinking. I had lots of shakes and I was coughing up blood.'

For David, salvation came in the shape of Alcoholics Anonymous. He had one drink after his first meeting in November 1995, but has not touched a drop since: 'I cannot say that it has been easy. In fact at times, the effects on my mind and body of quitting the booze have seemed worse than when I was a full-blown alcoholic. That drink after the first AA meeting could easily have seen me back on the rocky road – the temptation was, quite simply, that it would be much easier to start drinking than it would to stop. But I knew I had an equally simple choice: I either continued drinking and died, or stopped drinking and gave myself a chance of living.

'I have been incredibly lucky. My health is now perfect and amazingly my liver has not been damaged at all despite the abuse I put it through. I can only look forward to staying clean – and hope that I'll never be tempted to go back to the booze.'

IS ALCOHOL ALL BAD?

If you were to read, let alone believe, all the anti-alcohol press you could be forgiven for pouring your drink down the sink. After all, it's only a matter of time before it either sends you doolally, ruins your kids, kills you or all three.

However there is an equally vociferous pro-drink lobby who are all too pleased to promote the benefits of booze for a rounded, healthy lifestyle. Red wine, in particular, is singled out by doctors and enthusiasts alike if not as an elixir, then as a drink that you can at least enjoy without feeling too guilty. Certainly red wine is credited with easing stress and even reducing the risk of Alzheimer's – and it is, without doubt, proven to lower the risk of coronary heart disease, thanks to substances within it called flavonoids. 'There is mounting evidence to point to the flavonoids as being important contributory factors in the prevention of heart disease,' says Professor Catherine Rice-Evans, of Guy's Hospital in London. 'They might be acting as anti-oxidants and they might also be preventing certain cells in the blood from clumping together and causing a blockage. Drinking red wine with a healthy meal could also mean that the beneficial components you are eating get absorbed better.'

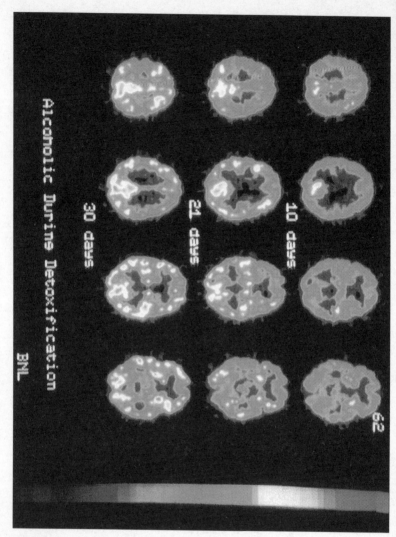

PET (Positron Emission Tomography) scans of horizontal slices of an alcoholic's brain during withdrawal. The front of the brain is at the top, and the slices get deeper from left to right. The brighter brain areas are those of high activity. The activity of the brain after (TOP-BOTTOM) 10 days, 21 days, and 30 days is seen. Brain activity is seen to increase after time spent without alcohol.

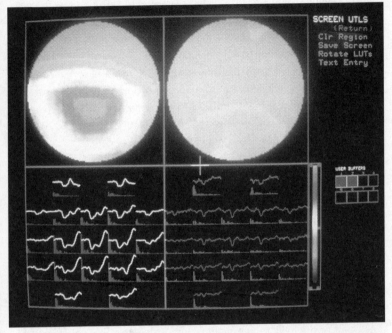

Evoked potential brain scan showing areas of electrical activity in a normal and alcoholic patient. LEFT: The brain of a normal patient, with high activity in the posterior region. RIGHT: The alcoholic patient shows depressed brain activity.

Meanwhile there is evidence to suggest that wine, unlike beer, does not make you fat. Researchers at Colorado State University asked 14 men with an average age of 30 to drink two glasses of red wine a day with their evening meal for six weeks, and then have no alcohol for six weeks. The results showed no tendency for the men to put on weight, even though the wine was in addition to normal food intake.

There is even evidence that wine can prevent the onset of Alzheimer's. Admittedly the scientists were from Bordeaux University in the heart of the French wine-growing country, but they nonetheless claimed that a survey of 4,000 people aged over 65 revealed four glasses of wine a day reduced the risk of developing the disease by 75 per cent.

Surveys come and surveys go, and to be honest they should all be taken with a pinch of salt – or at least not believed without first knowing who is supplying the funding. What does not seem to be in doubt, even among the anti-lobby, is that alcohol can be beneficial as long as it is taken in moderation. Indeed, it is argued that total abstinence can be worse for the body in the long term than a couple of glasses of wine a night. We have seen how wine can improve the chances of avoiding a heart attack, but another benefit of alcohol includes nutrition. Beer and wine not only contain minerals and trace elements such as zinc, copper, manganese and potassium, but many vitamins of the B group. A pint of beer provides 11 per cent of the daily requirement of pyridoxine, the vitamin which is of proved value in the treatment of pre-menstrual tension. Some wines and beer are such rich sources of potassium salts that they were often recommended, in the days before suitable supplements were available, for patients with renal and heart failure who were taking diuretics.

IS THERE HOPE? – 'CURES' FOR ALCOHOL

For years it had been the invention that everyone dreamed of: a pill that you could take at the end of a night's drinking that would instantly nullify the effects of alcohol – allowing you to drive home, wake up refreshed and eradicate the symptoms of dependency. In 1985, the drinking world held its breath as scientists at Hoffman-La Roche announced they were on the verge of discovering that very thing.

Called RO15-4513, this derivative of benzodiazepine was said to affect the brain's principal inhibitory neurotransmitter, a chemical called y(gamma)-aminobutyric acid (GABA) that controls the movement of chloride ions in the brain cells. The scientists had discovered that alcohol stimulates the GABA receptor to allow more chloride ions into the brain cells, thereby loosening inhibitions. But when RO15-4513 was introduced, it bound to the GABA receptor and blocked out any effect of alcohol. After only a few minutes, the drunk person would be sober again.

The big downfall with RO15-4513, however, was that it did not block out the effects of alcohol on the rest of the body. Thus the potentially deadly scenario was born of people drinking vast amounts of alcohol with no apparent effect, other than cirrhosis and heart disease. Faced with potentially ruinous lawsuits, pharmaceutical manufacturers refused to market the drug and RO15-4513 was quietly shelved.

In 1999, however, a radical new treatment for alcohol dependency emerged that allowed alcoholics to continue drinking. Developed by the National Public health Institute in Helsinki, the drug naltrexone blocks the receptors in the brain that normally respond to alcohol by producing endorphins, the body's natural opiates. This in turn dulls the effects of drinking and eventually weakens the body's cravings for alcohol. The treatment is aimed at patients who have not descended too far into alcoholism and are sufficiently motivated to get well. It cannot be given to patients whose livers have been seriously damaged by alcohol. In Finnish trials, 78 per cent of patients given the drug had still not relapsed after three years.

The ancient Greeks thought that eating cabbage would cure a hangover while the Romans thought that eating fried canaries would do the same. Today, some Germans eat a breakfast of red meat and bananas, some French drink strong coffee with salt, some Chinese drink spinach tea, some Puerto Ricans rub half a lemon under their drinking arm, some Haitians stick 13 black-headed needles into the cork of the bottle from which they drank, and some Russians drink vodka in an effort to cure hangovers. None of these 'cures' work.

Trials are still on-going, but there are those who claim that naltrexone merely removes the symptoms without treating the cause. Alcoholics continue to wait for the drug to become widely available...

> 'Ethyl alcohol is a colourless flammable liquid used to preserve fish.'
> – World Bank

FLEXING THEIR MUSCLES – THE ALCOHOL LOBBY

On their way to ousting the Conservative government in 1997, Tony Blair's New Labour made a number of promises. One that gained widespread support among the medical fraternity was Labour's avowed intent to lower the drink-drive limit from 80mg of alcohol per 100ml of blood to 50mg. On the face of it, the move made eminent sense. Lower limits have been shown to lower the number of drink-related deaths on the roads in countries like Australia, France, Sweden and Canada.

The fact that more than five years later the new limit shows no sign of being introduced is testament to the power of the UK alcohol lobby. There may be a wailing and gnashing of teeth about the perceived decline in traditional brewing, but the industry still has some powerful friends. Indeed, its power has arguably increased with the advent of multi-national drinks companies now taking control of the previously disparate and localized industry.

In Britain, the alcohol lobby consists largely of the brewers, distillers and other drinks manufacturers in tandem with various major organizations whose members rely upon the industry for their livelihood, such as the Federation of Small Businesses, the Road Haulage Association and the National Association of Local Councils. Together they wield substantial clout – as you might expect of an industry that employs over one million people (with its satellites), rakes in some

£53,000 ($78,026) of consumer money every minute and, most importantly, provides the Treasury with billions in taxable revenue. In the case of reducing the drink-driving limit, it was argued by the lobby that the proposed legislation would prove catastrophic to the already decimated rural pub business, which relies almost exclusively on people driving for bar meals in their cars. With the Labour government already stirring up the ire of the countryside brigade with their plans to ban fox-hunting, and with

President George W Bush knows first hand about alcohol addiction, undergoing a "faith-based" cure for his alcohol problem under the supervision of Billy Graham. The prelude to a meteoric political career.

members of the Countryside Alliance marching on Downing Street, it was obvious that a further knife in the back for rural life would be politically damaging. A Department of Transport report into the plan said, 'The consultation response shows very clearly the concerns of two overlapping interests about a lower limit: those of the alcohol industries and those of rural communities generally. Both are concerned primarily about the viability of rural pubs if a lower limit is adopted and properly enforced. Pubs and hotels can be a locally significant source of employment, and those in rural areas are particularly dependent on access by cars.'

It was not the first time that the best-laid plans had been scuppered by the alcohol lobby. Doctors have long been campaigning for a coherent national alcohol policy to help curb damage to health caused by alcohol abuse and to limit the potential for alcohol-related crime. In 1999 they produced a report, *Tackling Alcohol Together: Evidence Base For A UK Alcohol Policy*, and sat back to wait for the government to implement it. The report, of course, is still gathering dust. According to one of its authors, Dr Duncan Raistrick of the Leeds Addiction Unit, the reason for the prevarication is patently obvious. 'We have a world-class drinks industry,' he said. 'It is a very big dilemma, to be fair to politicians. There are very strong vested interests in making sure the supply of alcohol is not restricted.'

Of course, the government and the drinks industry have been partners in making money from alcohol since 1643, when Cromwell's parliament first imposed a levy on beer, and there is no reason to think that the partnership is going to dissolve now. However there may be a glimmer of hope for the campaigners. In 1843, it was decided that the Royal Navy's daily rum ration would be banned; the ban eventually became law – 134 years later – in 1968.

If anything, the alcohol lobby in the United States is more powerful than its UK equivalent. When proposals were put forward for a unified reduction in the US drink-driving limit in 1997, it barely left the planning stage before it was crushed beneath the weight of industry pressure, prompting one magazine to marvel at the influence of 'one of the most powerful and well-financed lobbying operations in Washington, a network of legal firms, lobbyists, and PR groups that jump when anyone rings the liquor bell.'

Since 1987, the US alcohol lobby – in particular the National Beer Wholesalers Association and the National Restaurant Association – has given an estimated $26 million (£17.7 million) in contributions to congressional candidates and 'soft money' contributions to national party committees. And the hand-outs have been evenly distributed, with some $16 million (£10.9 million) given to the Republican Party and $10 million (£6.8 million) to the Democrats.

Such generosity has demanded a pay back, and over the years the alcohol industry has won many battles in Congress. For example, it has been highly successful in combating attempts to increase federal taxes on its products. The lobby has also fended off attempts to increase taxes in order to pay for the impact of heavy drinking on society. In 1993, the Congressional Budget Office proposed substantial tax hikes in beer, spirits and wine to offset the cost of treating alcohol-related illness. But such was the power of the lobby that the proposals remained on paper only, with the Clinton administration ignoring them even as a way to pay for health care reform.

The lobby has also successfully scuppered plans to restrict alcohol advertising on TV. In 1996, Democrat Representative Joseph Kennedy sponsored legislation that would have placed restrictions on the advertising of alcoholic beverages in order to decrease young people's exposure to such ads. 'We spend $15 billion [(£10.2 billion)] In a war on drugs, but then allow an industry to tell young people if they want to get a pretty girl or win a bike race, they ought to go suck a brew,' Kennedy observed. The Kennedy proposal attracted just four co-sponsors and went nowhere; his other legislative proposals focused on alcohol advertising, including a Bill that would have banned all broadcast advertising of hard-liquor products, have also failed to leave the starting gate.

After the defeat of the drink-driving legislation, Brandy Anderson of the pressure group Mothers Against Drink Driving said the politicians were 'listening to the money. They did not act on the voice of America. Safety doesn't talk down here. Money talks.'

INDUSTRY WATCHDOGS – THE PORTMAN GROUP AND OTHERS

In 1989, in a bid to establish a degree of responsibility within its own membership, the UK alcohol industry launched the Portman Group, a pan-industry watchdog whose purpose is to help prevent the misuse of alcohol and promote sensible drinking. Portman is unique inasmuch as it has been set up by the industry itself. One of its primary activities is to monitor and prevent alcohol misuse by youngsters, admitting that the industry has to be seen to be doing something if it wants to retain its commercial freedom.

Despite initial suspicion that the watchdog would be rendered toothless by its creators, since its launch the Portman Group has been responsible for a number of important initiatives aimed at curbing teenage drinking. One of its first schemes was the Proof of Age card, designed for people aged 18 and over to be able to prove they are old enough to buy a drink. The criteria for getting one of the cards are tough – every applicant has to be sponsored by a 'responsible adult', such as a doctor, teacher or magistrate, and the age of every applicant is verified. But the fact that over 400,000 cards have so far been issued shows what a success it has become, especially for those fresh-faced 18-year-olds who look anything but.

Saying No To Underage Drinkers is a guide for staff in licensed premises and off-licences, which contains useful tips on how to 'refuse a potentially illegal sale without creating confrontation'. Tips include advice on being alert, standing your ground, avoiding blame and keeping your distance. Bearing in mind that many under age drinkers get their booze from the local corner shop, the guide is produced in Urdu, Punjabi, Gujerati and Hindi.

Discussing Drinking With Children is a general guide for parents who want information on talking to their children about alcohol – and again, it has proved popular not just with parents of teenagers, but parents of younger children too.

In the US, the alcohol industry does not have its own self-regulator as such, but the Marin Institute acts as a watchdog of alcohol marketing practices. What distinguishes their approach to the prevention of alcohol-related problems is that instead of focusing on individual risk factors, Marin concentrates on the environments that 'support and glamorize alcohol use'. In particular, it keeps a close eye on the one billion dollars spent annually by the US industry to advertise its products, and the increasingly powerful political clout it has in Washington. Similar groups are to be found in Europe: in Spain, one of the leading industry watchdogs has a reputation for taking manufacturers to court if they overstep the country's alcohol advertising guidelines.

CRYING INTO THEIR PINT POTS –
BREWING GIANTS AND THE SLOW DEATH OF BEER

There was a pall hanging over the 2001 Great British Beer Festival that, for once, had nothing to do with the hundreds of real ales that were being consumed below. Instead, beer aficionados were staring gloomily into their pints and wondering just how long the UK's premier brewing jamboree would continue.

The latest figures were out and beer consumption was at rock bottom thanks to the unprecedented rise in novelty cocktails, non-alcoholic health drinks and – those dreaded words – Drinks Multi-nationals. Between 1990 and 2000, consumption of beer in the UK had dropped by 13 per cent, to just 10 billion pints. Meanwhile Australia, long associated with hard-drinking

Ockers, had slumped from seventh to ninth place among beer-drinking nations, and South Africa Breweries reported a drastic collapse in the numbers of beer drinkers. Even the Germans, the world's biggest beer drinkers, were feeling the pinch with consumption dropping from 156 litres per head in the mid-1980s to just 125 litres – a lower *per capita* figure than the Czech Republic and Ireland.

And the news just got worse and worse. The country that gave the world modern brewing was being battered by foreign imports. In a market dominated by the likes of Bacardi Breezer and Smirnoff Ice, the only beer brands that numbered among the top sellers in the UK were internationally standardized varieties, especially premium lagers such as Interbrew's Stella Artois and Kronenbourg 1664.

The Campaign for Real Ale (Camra) continues to try to save individual pubs and prevent traditional British ales being swamped by bland Euro-fizz. And, in 2001, Prince Charles called for the traditional English pub to return to its roots as the focus of the community. But this is hardly cutting edge stuff in an era of multi-national brewing conglomerates with multi-million pound advertising budgets. Even as Prince Charles was campaigning for the return of the good old British pub Whitbread, which has been a brewing giant for more than 250 years, was offloading its 3,000-strong pub portfolio to Belgian multi-national Interbrew for £400 million ($589 million). Instead of producing beer, the company announced it was going to concentrate on restaurants, health clubs and hotels. In Germany Beck's, one of the best-regarded privately held brewers, was the subject of a takeover bid, again by Interbrew. Dozens of famous old brewing names have already fallen beneath the wheels of multi-national drinks giants...

'Beer has a global image problem,' says Peter Crean, of research firm AC Nielsen. 'Traditionally beer sells well when something is happening – new products, innovations. But not a lot is happening at the moment; you just get the same stuff everywhere you go. By contrast, young consumers are excited by the boom in snappily marketed bottled drinks, especially alcopops.'

But this is only part of the reason why the global brewing industry has shrunk to such an extent that just four companies now produce 80 per cent of all the beer drunk in Europe, while the rest is made up of American imports. The leisure sector has suffered as stockmarkets set their sights on high-growth technology stocks, with the pub trade suffering more than most. Meanwhile, high alcohol taxes have put pressure on even the biggest firms to squeeze margins.

The beer-dominated cultural landscape both in Britain and abroad has been changing for over 20 years. Beer sales worldwide have been falling since 1979 and show no sign of stopping. 'When you went into a pub in the 1970s, all there was to drink was beer,' says Mark Hastings, of the Brewers and Licensed Retailers Association (BLRA). 'Now there's a vastly wider choice of drinks.'

It's a fair point, but it doesn't explain why beer has been suffering, in retail terms, a slow, lingering death. There is another factor to take into consideration. Compared to exciting new products like alcopops, beer has a severe image problem. To the new generation of drinkers, real ale is something their fat old dads drink down the pub. If you drink anything out of a pint glass these days, it's got to be ice-cold Euro lager in a loud, strobe-lit designer bar. Mostly, though, beer equals Budweiser.

According to the writer Matthew Engel, 'The present generation of young drinkers is the most credulous, malleable and undiscerning ever. This is the generation who, as kids, forced their parents to buy them rip-off football shirts and plimsolls, marketed as overpriced fashion

> The cost to the NHS of Britain's drinking habits is as high as £3 billion ($4.92 billion) a year, according to a report published in March 2002 by Alcohol Concern for a conference of GPs and other professionals who work in primary care.

items. Now they're older, they appear to be suckers for tasteless beer in tasteless bars.' Engel continues, 'This lot would drink their granny's widdle if some smart-arse copywriter came up with a line that persuaded them into thinking it was a fresh, exotic and sexy sort of lager. Heaven knows what they will turn to next. But I predict the first half of the 21st century will be vintage years for snake oil salesmen, political demagogues and evangelical maniacs.'

'I BET HE DRINKS CARLING BLACK LABEL' –
ALCOHOL ADVERTISING

Whatever the brand, alcohol is big business and the rewards for cornering the market can be worth billions to the manufacturers. So it is understandable that when it comes to advertising, no expense is spared in hiring the best creative talent in the industry. In 2000, £227.3 million ($334.6 million) was spent on alcohol advertising in the UK alone, a figure matched by most European countries but one which is simply dwarfed by the $1 billion (£679 million) spent annually by the American brewing giants.

The results, in terms of the cultural landscape, have been far reaching. Advertising campaigns, for often unspectacular alcoholic products, have been etched so indelibly on the public consciousness that some have even become part of the language. Meanwhile the characters dreamed up by ad companies to promote the product have evolved into a life of their own. Some classics include...

- **Budweiser** – The American giant was always going to have to go some to top their legendary Budweiser frog campaign – but they did it seamlessly by introducing a gang of beer-swilling, sports-watching slackers who spent their time shouting 'Whassssuuuuppp!' to each other. Simple, annoying, but very funny and very effective.
- **Carling Black Label** – A bog-standard lager became a national obsession in Britain, thanks to an advertising campaign featuring TV comics The Oblivion Brothers, and coined the phrase 'I bet he drinks Carling Black Label'. The most famous commercial spoofed the war film *The Dambusters*, and showed two Lancaster bomber pilots dropping a series of bouncing bombs on a German dam and the sentry on duty catching them goalkeeper-style.
- **Castlemaine XXXX** – 'He who thinks Australian drinks Australian' is the tagline of this continuing series of witty commercials for the Aussie lager. In one of the later examples, an Ocker layabout has been sleeping with his best friend's wife, but when she offers him a can of XXXX he is mortally offended that she would hand him another man's beer.

- **Foster's** - Never straying far from his successful Crocodile Dundee persona, Aussie comic Paul Hogan fronted a series of ads between 1984 and 1990 in which an uncomplicated Ocker took solace in the 'Amber Nectar' when confronted by a series of unusual situations. A typical example saw Hogan at the ballet, startled to see a male dancer in tights. 'Strewth,' he exclaims, 'there's a bloke down there with no strides on!'.

- **Grolsch** - The profile of this distinctive Dutch beer was raised by a series of ads featuring a laid-back Netherlander interrupting a series of events - including a wedding and a pornographic movie - with his catchphrase 'Schtop!' The idea that people should take time and relax, just like the brewers of Grolsch.

- **Guinness** - From the early days of billboards claiming that 'Guinness Is Good For You', the Dublin-based company have always understood the importance of brand awareness in the market. A series of ads produced in the 1990s have become advertising benchmarks, including one featuring a line of white horses apparently emerging from a raging surf, which was voted No.1 in British TV show entitled *100 Great TV Ads*.

- **Heineken** - This campaign introduced the ultimate advertising pay-off line 'Heineken refreshes the parts other beers cannot reach', which grabbed the public imagination so much it was eventually included in the 1998 edition of the *Oxford Dictionary Of Modern Quotations*. Launched in 1974, there were over 100 ads in the campaign that won over 300 creative awards along the way. An all-time favourite featured the poet William Wordsworth stumbling through a field of daffodils, muttering 'I walked about a bit on my own'. After swigging from a can of Heineken he uttered the immortal lines, 'I wandered lonely as a cloud...'

- **Holsten Pils** - Pinching an idea from the Steve Martin movie *Dead Men Don't Wear Plaid*, the most famous Holsten campaign featured British comic Griff Rhys Jones superimposed into a number of classic movies. In one commercial, he was seen extolling the virtues of the lager to Marilyn Monroe in a scene from *Some Like It Hot*.

Three ladies, wearing traditional flamboyant headwear, enjoying a traditional drink of Pimms on the second day of Royal Ascot. As a group, young women demonstrate the fastest-growing levels of alcohol consumption. In the UK, the number of women over-indulging had risen from 9 per cent in 1984 to 16 per cent in 2000. In Australia, a recent survey revealed that 31 per cent of women aged 23–28 binge drink, with the number rising to 70 per cent for 18–23-year-olds. In the US, it is estimated that 66 per cent of all women drink, and the alcohol-related death rate there now matches that of Europe (5 per 100,000 population), although in certain eastern European countries the figure is three times higher.

Why are women drinking more? 'Stress and increased spending power are seen as major factors – but this overlooks the fact that we also drink because it is utterly enjoyable, a wonderful way to unwind and counteract shyness. It's a fast escape, a short holiday. Women's lives are so consumed by juggling work and family that they need quick thrills to squeeze into limited free time. Alcohol fits the bill perfectly.' (Novelist Laura Hird)

In the USA, a voluntary ban on advertising hard spirits on TV has existed since 1948, when alcohol manufacturers and broadcasters agreed to restrict the use of commercials. However, in recent years companies such as Seagram and Bacardi have advertised on small local and cable channels. And now alcohol advertising is beginning to return to US TV stations as broadcasters that are desperate to boost revenues are swallowing their principles. In 2001, the Distilled Spirits Council of the United States rewrote its code of good practice to allow its member distillers to advertise on radio and television. Soon after that, distilling giant Brown-Forman announced its biggest-ever advertising campaign to promote its Jack Daniels whisky brand.

As well as the billions of pounds spent every year on traditional TV, radio and newspaper commercials, manufacturers are spending an increasing amount of time and creativity exploring the global marketing potential of the Internet in a bid to secure the loyalty of the new generation of computer-literate drinkers and capitalize on the web's strong and unique attraction for young people.

Some of the techniques used to hook young drinkers are wickedly effective, especially those used by US-based manufacturers. The Center for Media Education (CME) noted the following examples.

- The Budweiser online radio network, KBUD, hosted by DJ BuddyK, which intersperses music and pop interviews with a steady stream of beer promotions.
- Interactive games like Molson's *Berserk In Banff*, or the Cuervo *JC Roadhog Adventure*, in which a red cyber-rodent zooms through a desert littered with tequila bottles and other Cuervo merchandise.
- Branded merchandise and free giveaways, including clothing, beer mugs, screen savers and screen wallpaper decked out with company logos.
- Heavy promotion of alcopops on sites including contests for the best recipe.
- Virtual communities based on the product brand, such as Cuervo's 'Republic of Cuervo Gold', where inhabitants can 'separate from our

fears, our blues, and our cares, as we enter the doors of our favourite establishment in search of frivolity – and perhaps a margarita or two'.

- Brand characters, such as Capt Morgan (of Capt Morgan Rum), and Budbrew J Budfrog (of Budweiser Beer) – the latter 'drives a luxury German car, has memorized the entire *Oxford English Dictionary*, and likes to lie on the beach with a hot babe, a cold Bud, and a folio edition of the *Kama Sutra* in its original Sanskrit'.
- Online magazines and marketing surveys, like the Schlager website's extensive survey where visitors are encouraged to 'Take the Golschlager Fan test and as a reward we'll give you a 30 per cent discount off any Goldschlager Gear from our Gear Catalogue'.
- Ongoing fiction, such as Moet & Chandon's web-novel about 20-something New Yorkers who meet up to flirt, have sex, gossip and, most importantly, quaff Moet champagne.

Advertising in the form of sports sponsorship has also proved to be hugely effective for the drink manufacturers, with high-profile sports like soccer in Europe and gridiron and baseball in the US receiving a sizeable chunk of the estimated £100 billion ($147.2 billion) spent every year by alcohol companies. Indeed sport has come to rely so heavily upon the annual hand-out from its sponsors that when the UK pressure group Alcohol Concern called for restrictions, claiming a link with excessive drinking among youngsters, the government rejected the argument fearing it could cause financial problems for teams and events and therefore prove hugely unpopular with fans.

In the US, Anheuser-Busch is the main sponsor of sports. In Europe, the big players include:

- Warsteiner (among others, it sponsors the European Skiing Federation);
- Amstel (soccer's Champion's League);
- United Distillers (Johnny Walker golf tournament);
- Berry, Bros & Co (the Cutty Sark regatta);
- Carlsberg (sponsors the European Football Championships, the International Amateur Athletics Federation, the Athletics World Championships and Liverpool FC).

WHITE VAN MAN – THE CROSS-CHANNEL BOOZE BANDITS

'I'm a firm believer that duty should be put down. I'm doing all I can to ensure people break the law, like they did with the poll tax.' So says Dave West, owner of EastEnders, one of the most lucrative alcohol outlets in France. Situated on a ringroad outside Calais, EastEnders is a huge warehouse full to the rafters with cut-price booze designed specifically for sale to the thousands of Brits who cross the Channel every week in order to load up their vans. The law allows travellers within the European Union to take back to their country almost as many drinks as they like for personal consumption, with a limit of 110 litres of beer or 90 litres of wine.

Current statistics in Norway indicate that 80 per cent of crimes of violence, 60 per cent of rapes, arson and vandalism are committed under the influence of alcohol.

But the term 'personal consumption' has proved to be a grey area when it comes to getting more than that past customs in the UK. It has also become a highly profitable loophole for professional smugglers, who then sell off the drink once they reach the white cliffs. Customs reckons that over £200 million ($294.4 million) of revenue is lost to Britain through alcohol smuggling each year – and with entrepreneurs like Dave West, not to mention the dozens of other British-run outlets, only too happy to supply his fellow countrymen with as much booze as they can carry, the problem is not going to go away easily.

Smuggling is not just a headache for the taxman. It is estimated that of the 1.4 million pints of beer brought across the Channel each day, 75 per cent are destined for resale. 'Our Kent pubs have lost a quarter of their business because of imported beer from Calais,' says Stuart Neame, deputy chairman of real ale producer Shepherd Neame. 'Traditional farmworkers and locals used to go to the pub five or six times a week. Now they have a stock of cheap beer at home and drink it in front of the television.'

Steps have been taken to remedy the situation. There are now several thousand 'excise verification officers' patrolling Dover docks in order to stop and search suspicious vehicles to establish whether their supply is for personal use and, if not, demand proof that the alcohol is destined for a party or a special event. To get round this inconvenience, some professional bootleggers now make fake bookings at church halls. And, with an estimated 27,000 people involved in smuggling, the job of the customs officials seems even more fruitless.

'Freddie Laker got a knighthood for getting air fares down,' says the unrepentant Dave West. 'I'm doing what I can to get taxes down.'

ADDITIONAL INFO

'When I read about the evils of drinking, I gave up reading.'

~ Henny Youngman (1906-98)

You may not speak the language, you may not understand the culture – but, wherever you are in the world tonight, you will be able to get a drink. So order yourself a large one as we attempt to summarize the alcohol story.

If there is one constant in mankind's fluctuating history, it is alcohol. It has been with us during war and peace, it has dictated economies and policies and it has subjugated great powers and brought their conquerors crashing down. Alcohol is our best friend and our own worst enemy, a comfort and a killer. It is a drug that few care to be without and only the foolish attempt to ban, for as long as there is human civilization, as long as there is the natural process of fermentation, alcohol will be an intrinsic part of our lives.

In 21st-century Britain, the political debate is dominated by the pros and cons of 'joining' Europe. Yet modern, airy bars stacked with continental beers that now jostle for custom in the city centres are proof that it has already happened. The smoky, male-dominated pubs and clubs that were once such a part of insular Britain's cultural landscape are now firmly in its dim and distant history. Women are welcomed and actively targeted, where before they either pulled the pints or collected the glasses. The modern drinker does not want to drink in the same pub as his or her parents. Behind the backs of the policy makers the new generation have welcomed Europe by embracing its drinking culture.

Health campaigners may quite rightly fret about binge drinking and drink-related violence among young people – but bingeing and scrapping are surely the last remaining symptoms of licensing laws laid down almost half a century ago, when the world was a different place. Once these arcane restrictions are scrapped, and people are allowed to drink when and where they choose, they will no longer find the '11-o'clock swill' either necessary or desirable. It may yet take a few years before Britain is as comfortable and civilized with alcohol as most of its European cousins are, but it is surely the way forward.

The Americans may have further to go. Seventy years after Prohibition it is a country still wracked with guilt about drinking, yet paralyzed by a stalemate between the temperance lobby on one side and the alcohol lobby on the other. The result is an unsatisfactory limbo in which American teenagers are bombarded by sophisticated alcohol advertising yet cannot legally buy a drink until they are 21. It is amazing that people are surprised at the levels of illicit boozing going on in the high schools and university campuses. And it seems astonishing that the lesson of Prohibition – that the greater the restriction, the more people will drink – has not been learned. But while it would be tempting to say that the solution lies in a more relaxed 'European' approach to alcohol, US administrations are utterly hamstrung by their need to keep both lobbies sweet.

Of course, Europe is by no means a uniformly perfect model of how to live with alcohol. Certain former Soviet Bloc countries are, in places, reminiscent of England during the gin epidemic of the 1700s – only this time the drink is moonshine vodka. Here the case is most definitely for governments to step up the laws rather than relax them. In Scandinavia, meanwhile, hard drinking continues at heroic levels despite punitive prices. Even France, which was for so long held up as a paragon of sophisticated alcohol consumption, tops the league of cirrhosis victims. They may be able to hold their drink, but they drink more of it than anyone else in the world and suffer accordingly.

Alcohol is a highly toxic poison and so the health debate essentially boils down to a simple fact: drink too much and it will eventually kill you. Another fact is that however dire the warnings, certain people will always drink too much – in the same way that some people will always gamble too much, smoke too much or take too many drugs. It is fatuous to blame alcohol for something that is most probably genetic. But it is worth remembering that, of the billions of people who will take a drink tonight, only a tiny fraction have a 'problem' with it.

Alcohol highlights natural characteristics that would ordinarily be strangled by inhibition. In 95 per cent of cases these characteristics include wit, wisdom, compassion, comradeship, love. In an often drab and humourless world, this is surely something worth raising a glass to.

GLOSSARY

Absinthe – spirit drink made with aromatics including star anise, fennel seed, and crushed wormwood leaves. It is green in colour but turns white when water is added to it.

Alcohol: Ethyl alcohol or ethanol, is the type found in alcohol beverages. But the term is also commonly used to refer to alcohol beverages in general. The word alcohol is from the Arabic 'al kohl', which means 'the essence'.

Ale – style of beer made with a top-fermenting yeast. Ales are typically hearty, robust and fruity.

Amaretto – liqueur with a slightly bitter almond flavour, made from apricot pips.

Amontillado – nutty dry sherry that is produced in Spain.

Anisette – fragrant liqueur, made with anise seeds, that has a liquorice flavour.

Anjou – white wine from the Loire Valley of France.

Anti-Saloon League – major organization involved in bringing about national Prohibition in the US. It is now known as the American Council on Alcohol Problems, as it has been combined with the American Temperance League. This group actively attempts to influence public policy.

Aperitif – alcohol beverage typically flavoured with herbals such as fruits, seeds, flowers or herbs.

Appellation contrôlleé – French system introduced in 1855 that was designed to regulate the variety of grapes, quantity produced and geographic origin of wines that bear a specific place name, such as Champagne or Chablis.

Applejack – sweet apple-flavoured brandy.

Aqua vitae or 'water of life' – original name given to distilled spirits, which were first made for medicinal and health purposes.

Armagnac – grape brandy produced in the Gers district of Southern France. It is aged in hard, black oak from Gascony.

BAC – abbreviation for blood alcohol content or the proportion of alcohol in a person's blood.

Bacchus – mythological god who was said to have spread wine culture throughout Europe.

Balthazar – large bottle that holds 12 litres or the equivalent of 16 standard bottles of champagne.

Barrel – standard unit of volume. A US barrel is 31.5 gallons while a British barrel is 43.2 gallons.

Beaujolais – light, fruity red wine produced in the Beaujolais region of France.

Beaujolais nouveau – light red wine from the Beaujolais region of France that is released after a few weeks of fermentation.

Beer – fermented beverage made from barley malt or other cereal grains. The name comes from the Latin 'bibere' (meaning 'to drink'). Lager beer is a light, dry beer. Ale is heavier and more bitter than lager. Bock beer, porter and stout are progressively heavier, darker, richer and sweeter.

Belgian lace – white pattern of foam from the head of beer that is left on a glass after the beverage has been consumed.

Binge drinking – consumption by a male of five drinks in a row and a woman of four.

Bitters – type of aperitif or cordial with a bitter taste used primarily to flavour mixed drinks.

Bock – strong lager beer traditionally brewed to celebrate the approach of spring. Bocks are typically full-bodied, malty and well-hopped.

Bordeaux – wine-growing region in southwestern France. It includes Medoc, Pomerol, St. Emilion and Sauternes.

Bottom fermentation – occurs when *saccharomyces carlsbergensis* ('lager yeast') is used in fermentation because this strain of yeast settles to the bottom of a tank during the process.

Bourbon – spirit that is distilled from a mash of at least 51 per cent corn and is then aged in new charred oak barrels. It was first produced by Reverend Elijah Craig in Bourbon County, Kentucky.

Brandy – spirit that is distilled from wine or fermented fruit mash. The word comes from the Dutch 'brandewijn', meaning burnt (or distilled) wine.

Breathalyzer – device used to measure blood alcohol concentration by measuring the alcohol content of a person's exhaled breath.

Brown ale – British-style, top-fermented beer that is lightly hopped and flavoured with roasted and caramel malt.

Brut – dry Champagne.

Burgundy – wine district in France. The term is also generically used to refer to other wines that resemble those produced in Burgundy.

Cabernet sauvignon – most produced and used red grape variety in the world.

Calvados – apple brandy distilled from cider in the town of the same name in northern France where it is produced.

Cassis – purple liqueur made from currants.

Chablis – dry white wine made from Chardonnay grapes in the Chablis region of France. It is also used generically to refer to other wines that resemble the wine produced in Chablis.

Champagne – effervescent wine made in the Champagne region of France, generally blended from several different years and from as many as 40 different wines. Occasionally a vintage is of such a superior quality that a vintage Champagne is produced. Sparkling wines from other areas of the world are sometimes generically labelled champagne, but increasingly producers elsewhere are now correctly and accurately labelling such wine as 'sparkling wine'.

Châteauneuf-du-Pape – 'new castle of the Pope' is a village in the Rhone valley of France whose red wines are made from Grenache and Syrah grapes.

Chardonnay – white grape variety that is widely planted around the world and can produce fine wine.

Chenin Blanc – versatile white grape variety widely grown in California and South Africa.

Chianti – wine from the Tuscany region of Italy.

Cider – this is unfermented apple juice in the US but fermented apple juice in the rest of the world. (In the US, fermented apple juice is called hard cider.)

Claret – dry red wine from the Bordeaux region of France.

Congeners – refers to the taste and flavour elements in alcohol beverages.

Cognac – brandy distilled from wine in the Cognac region of France. This means that all cognac is brandy but not all brandy is cognac.

Cooler – beverage made with a base of beer, wine or spirits combined with ingredients such as fruit or cocktail flavours.

Cru – grape production from a French vineyard.

Curacao – cordial that is flavoured with sour orange peel.

Cuvee – large vat used for fermentation.

Demi-sec – moderately sweet to medium sweet sparking wines.

Designated driver – person who does not drink at an event in order to drive others home.

Digestif – French for liqueur.

Distilled spirits – ethanol that is produced by heating fermented products, such as wine or mash, and then condensing the resulting vapours. This is sometimes referred to as liquor or hard liquor.

DOC – abbreviation for Denominazione di Origine Controllata, or 'controlled place name'. This is Italy's designation for wine whose name, origin of grapes, grape varieties and other important factors are regulated by law. It is also the abbreviation for Portugal's highest wine category, and has the same meaning in that country.

Draught beer – keg beer that is served on tap.

Drink-driving – driving a vehicle while under the influence of alcohol (UK term).

Dry – absence of sugar or sweetness in a beverage. It also refers to political subdivisions or areas in which the sale of alcohol is prohibited or to individuals who advocate prohibition.

Eggnog – beverage made with milk, whole eggs, nutmeg and dark rum.

Enology (or oenology) – science and art of wine making, also known as viniculture.

Extra dry – when referring to sparkling wines, this actually means sweet.

Fermentation – process during which yeast converts sugar into alcohol and carbon dioxide.

Fortified wine – wine to which alcohol has been added to increase the proof to a higher level than the maximum possible from fermentation.

Gamay – red grape variety well known for its use in making Beaujolais wines.

Genever – see *Gin*.

Gill – unit of measurement equivalent to 142g (5oz). British soldiers used to be guaranteed a ration of two gills of gin or rum each day during the Anglo-Dutch wars of 1652–74.

Gin – distilled spirit flavoured with juniper berries. It may also include additional flavourings. First made by the Dutch, gin was called junever, which is the Dutch word for juniper. The French called it genievre, which the English changed to geneva and then modified this to gin.

Grappa – Italian brandy made from pomace, which refers to the seeds and skins that remain after wine making.

Grenadine – non-alcoholic syrup made from a variety of fruits and used to flavour alcoholic drinks.

Grog – rum diluted with water. Also an early English name for Caribbean rum.

Hangover – unpleasant consequence of consuming too much alcohol. It is characterized by headache, fatigue and often nausea.

Highballs – made with almost any distilled spirit, ice, and any of a number of carbonated beverages.

Hogshead – 60-gallon oak barrel.

Hops – Small, cone-shaped flowers of a vine (*humulus lupulus*). Some varieties contribute mainly bitterness to brews, while others contribute aromas. Hops were originally used to preserve beer.

ICAP – Abbreviation of the International Council on Alcohol Policies, which is a public interest organization that seeks to reduce the abuse of alcohol worldwide.

India pale ale – Originally an ale brewed in England for British troops stationed in India during the 1700s. It was brewed very strong to survive a voyage that could last as long as six months and was also highly hopped to help preserve it.

Irish whiskey – Triple-distilled, blended grain spirits from Ireland.

Jeroboam – Large bottle that holds 3 litres of champagne.

Julep – drink traditionally made from Kentucky bourbon and fresh mint leaves, although it can be made with gin, rye, brandy, brandy, rum or champagne.

Keg – measure of volume. A keg of beer contains 56kg (1,984oz).

Lager – beer made with bottom-fermented yeast, and which is generally smooth and crisp.

Legal drinking age – minimum age at which alcohol beverages may legally be consumed.

Legs – streams of liquid that cling to the sides of a glass after the contents have been swirled. Commonly believed to be an indicator of quality, there is little evidence to support this belief. Also known as 'tears'.

Liebfraumilch – means 'milk of the virgin' and is a blended white German wine.

Light beer – reduced-calorie beer that is created by removing dextrine, a tasteless carbohydrate.

Liqueur – sugared and flavoured distilled spirit.

Liquor – historically referred to any alcohol beverage but today the term generally refers only to distilled spirits.

London dry gin – unsweetened gin.

MADD – Mothers Against Drunk Driving, an organization that strongly and actively opposes driving after the consumption of any alcohol.

Maceration – process of placing crushed fruit into distilled spirits for a period of time in order to impart the flavour of the fruit.

Madeira – dessert wine made on the Portuguese island of the same name.

Magnum – bottle holding 1.5 litres or the equivalent of two regular bottles of champagne.

Malt (or malted barley) – barley that has been moistened, allowed to germinate, then dried.

Mash – ground malt (germinated barley) mixed with water.

Mead – beverage made by fermenting honey mixed with water.

Moonshine – illegally produced, potent distilled alcohol that is usually concocted in home-made stills and made from anything – from wheat through to potatoes.

Mountain dew – another name for moonshine.

Nebuchadnezzar – large champagne bottle holding 15 litres or the contents of 20 standard bottles.

Neutral spirit – ethyl alcohol of 190 proof or higher that has no taste of the grains or fruits from which it was made.

Noble rot – another name for the *botrytis cinerea* mold that can pierce grape skins to cause dehydration. The resulting grapes produce a highly prized sweet wine.

Oktoberfest – beer festival held annually in Munich for 16 days and nights in late September and early October, originally held to celebrate a royal wedding in 1810.

Ouzo – anise-flavoured, brandy-based Greek liqueur.

Phylloxera vatatrex – microscopic underground insect that kills grape vines by attacking their roots. The insects destroyed virtually all of Europe's vineyards in the last quarter of the 19th century. Therefore, today virtually all of Europe's grape vines are grafted onto the roots of American grape varieties that are resistant to the destructive insects.

Pinot Blanc – white grape whose wine is often blended with Chardonnay.

Pinot Gris – greyish-rose coloured grape that can produce full-bodied white wines.

Pinot Noir – red wine grape that is important in the Burgundy region of France.

Pomace – the skins and seeds that remain after making wine.

Port – fortified dessert wine from Oporto, Portugal.

Porter – very dark, top-fermented beer.

Prohibition – legal attempt to prevent the production and the consumption of alcoholic beverages.

Proof – alcohol content of a beverage.

Punch – drink mixture prepared in large quantities that is typically made with citrus juices and two or more wines or distilled spirits. Carbonated beverages are often included. Hot punches may use milk, eggs and cream as a base.

Qualitätswein – designation of better-quality German wines.

Rehoboam – large champagne bottle holding 4.5 litres or the equivalent of six regular bottles.

Retsina – wine flavoured with pine resin, a very popular beverage in Greece.

Rice wine – see *Saké*.

Root beer – non-alcoholic beverage that was developed by temperance activists in the hope that it would replace real beer in popularity.

Rosé wines – red wines that have not been permitted to have long contact with the skins of the red grapes from which they are made.

Ruby – port that is generally sweet.

Rum – beverage distilled from fermented molasses.

Rye whiskey – whiskey that is distilled from a mash of at least 51 per cent rye grain.

Saké – fermented drink made from rice that is very popular in Japan. Although commonly called rice wine, it is actually a beer.

Salmanazar – large champagne bottle that holds 9 litres or the equivalent of 12 regular bottles.

Sambuca – Italian liquorice-flavoured liqueur made from elderberries, often ignited as part of a pub drinking game.

Sangria – punch made from red wine along with orange, lemon and apricot juice plus sugar.

Sauternes – sweet wine made in the Bordeaux region of France that is created from grapes infected with noble rot.

Schnapps – spirit distilled from potatoes or grain, called schnapps in Scandinavian countries and Germany but known as vodka elsewhere.

Scotch whisky – blend of whiskies generally aged up to ten years (about four years on average) with a characteristic smoky flavour resulting from drying malted barley over peat fires.

Sherry – fortified wine that has been subjected to controlled oxidation to produce a distinctive flavour.

Shiraz – Australian name for the Syrah grape.

Shooter – mixed drink served straight up in a small glass to be swallowed in one gulp.

Single malt Scotch whisky – Unblended Scotch whisky. They vary substantially in character depending on the mash from which they are made but all exhibit the unique smoky flavour of any Scotch whisky.

Sloe gin – not gin but a brandy-based cordial made from sloe berries (the fruit of blackthorn bushes).

Sour mash whiskey – whiskey made from a mash containing about 25 per cent residue from a previous mash, providing additional character to the resulting drink.

Sparkling wine – carbonated wine.

Speakeasy – establishment in which people could consume illegal alcohol beverages during national Prohibition in the US (1920–33). The name derived from the fact that people often had to whisper a code word or name through a slot in a locked door in order to gain admittance. Also referred to as a blind pig.

Stout – very dark, heavy, top-fermented beer.

Tannin – naturally occurring astringent acid found in many alcohol beverages that imparts a slight dry 'puckering' sensation in the mouth.

Teetotaller – person who abstains from alcohol.

Temperance – generally, abstinence and prohibition of alcohol.

Tequila – distilled from the Mescal Blue or Tequilana Weber agave plant in Mexico.

Toasting – tradition said to have started in ancient Rome, when a piece of toasted bread was dropped into the beverage.

Top fermentation – occurs when *saccharomyces cerevisiae* ('ale yeast') is used in fermentation. This strain of yeast rises to the top of a tank during fermentation. See also *bottom fermentation*.

Triple sec – cordial flavoured with the bittersweet oils of orange peels.

Varietal wine – wine that is made primarily from one variety of grape.

Vermouth - wine that has been soaked with as many as 40 flavourful aromatic herbs and spices.

Vintage - technically means harvest. When a vintage year is indicated on a label, it signifies that all the grapes used to make the wine in the bottle were harvested in that year. Except in the case of French Champagnes, vintage is not a clear indicator of quality.

Viniculture - see *Enology*.

Vinification - process of making grape juice into wine.

Viticulture - cultivation of grapes. Not to be confused with viniculture.

Vodka - Russian beverage distilled from potatoes or grain (usually corn and wheat).

WCTU - Abbreviation of the Women's Christian Temperance Union, an organization that was pivotal in bringing about national Prohibition in the US.

Wheat beer - Produced from a mash that includes wheat. The resulting beer varies from light and fruity in the US to a dark bock in Germany.

Whiskey - spirit distilled from grain in the US, Canada, or Ireland (note the spelling - compare to whisky entry).

Whisky - spirit distilled from grain in Scotland.

White lightning - another name for moonshine, or illegally produced distilled spirits.

Wine - fermented juice of grapes.

Wort - sweet liquid mash extract that is food for yeast and produces alcohol and carbon dioxide.

Zinfandel - red grape variety widely planted in California although it is not, contrary to common belief, native to that state.

Zymurgy - science and art of brewing.

ALCOHOL TIMELINE

c8,000 BC: A fermented, mead-like drink is produced from honey and wild yeasts in Persia and the Middle East.

c6,000 BC: Evidence of early wine production is found in an area south of the Russian Caucasus between the Black Sea and the Caspian Sea.

c4,000 BC: Wine making is established in Mesopotamia – present-day Iraq.

c3,000 BC: Wine making begins in ancient Egypt; slaves are fed porridge-like beer made from barley. Recipes for over 20 varieties of beer are recorded on clay tablets.

1,750 BC: The Babylonian Code of Hammurabi reveals that beer drinking is as common as wine drinking. Hammurabi spells out punishments for those who sell short measures.

c1,000 BC: Both the Etruscan and the Greek civilizations begin to cultivate wine. Large-scale vineyards are laid out in Assyria.

c800 BC: The distillation of barley and rice beer is practised in India.

200 BC: The Romans begin to cultivate wine in southern Italy; the Greeks name the country Enotria, or 'land of wine'.

51 BC: Romans invade Britain and discover tribal chiefs have stocks of wine imported from the continent.

50 BC: Dionysus of Halicarnassus writes, 'The Gauls have no knowledge of wine...but used a foul-smelling liquor made of barley rotted in water (beer).'

1st century AD: In his *Natural History*, Pliny writes the first wine 'manual'.

AD 400: Due to Roman influence, wine is now introduced to almost every European region.

AD 500: Wine making reaches China along the Silk Road.

AD 610: St Columbus begins exporting wine from Nantes to Ireland. The Angles, Saxons and Jutes introduce copious amounts of beer and cider to Britain.

AD 768: First specific reference to the use of hops in beer at Abbey St Denis in France.

AD 982: King Aethelred of Britain imposes a toll on wine entering the country from Rouen. King Howell of Wales introduces rules for the manufacture of mead.

1100: Alcohol distillation is documented by the medical school at Salerno, Italy. The product of the distillation is named 'spirits' in reference to it being the extracted spirit of the wine.

1151-2: A disastrous wine harvest means the French are forced to drink beer and mead.

1157: Thomas-á-Becket makes a gift of Canterbury ale to the French King.

1200: Arab alchemists manage to separate ethyl alcohol from beverages.

1213: The first cargo of Gascon wine arrives in Southampton.

1215: The *Magna Carta* includes a clause about the standard measures for ale and wine.

1267: The Assize of Bread and Ale is introduced by Henry III, which controls the price of these two staple items.

1276: The first ale 'conners' are introduced in London to keep a check on the quality of ale.

1307: Edward I dies of dysentery while fighting the Scots. He is given wine to drink as a possible cure. Distillation of grain alcohol in Europe follows the earlier distillation of wine.

1400: The Mistery of Free Brewers established in London.

1437: The Worshipful Company of Brewers is granted a charter by Henry VI. Hops begins to be used for brewing in England for the first time.

1496: The burghers of Nuremberg forbid the sale of 'distilled' waters on high days and holidays to stem the tide of drunkenness.

1516: The German Beer Purity Law (*Rheinheitsgebot*) makes it illegal to make beer with anything but barley, hops and pure water.

Benedictine, a cognac-based alcohol with added herbs, is developed at Fecamp monastery, Normandy.

The term alcohol is now used specifically to refer to distilled spirits rather than its previous general meaning of any product of the process of vaporizing and condensing.

1525: *The Vertuose Boke Of Dystyllacion Of The Waters Of All Manner Of Herbes* is published in Britain, revealing many health-giving recipes for alcohol.

1583: Queen Elizabeth allows the Vintners' Company to impose fines on vintners employing anyone who has not served a proper apprenticeship in the guild.

1638: The Distillers' Company is formed in London.

1643: Britain imposes a tax on distilled spirits.

1689: William of Orange comes to the throne and relaxes distilling tax and other regulations.

1720-50: The gin epidemic sweeps London.

1736: The ineffective Gin Act is introduced in England.

1751: Punitive taxation is introduced on spirits and severe penalties placed on illegal distillers in a bid to curb the gin epidemic.

1756: The Gin Tax is increased. Major beer breweries begin to be established.

1791: The Whiskey Tax is introduced the USA, placing duty on both publicly and privately distilled whiskey. (See p167)

1793: The Whiskey Rebellion of Pennsylvania occurs, during which government troops arrest a handful of dissident distillers.

1802: Thomas Jefferson repeals the Whiskey Tax.

1803: The first temperance group is set up in the US.

1814-17: A new alcohol tax is imposed in the US to help pay for the War of 1812.

1829: John Edgar launches the Ulster Temperance Society.

1830: Wellington introduces his disastrous Sale of Beer Act. Beer shops proliferate, as does drunkenness. Gin Palaces begin opening. The London Temperance Society is created.

1838: Father Mathew launches his anti-alcohol campaign.

1850: Prohibition is introduced in Maine, USA.

1860: The first Food and Drugs Act is introduced to curb the adulteration of beer.

1869: The British Wine and Beer-House Act makes it necessary to obtain a licence from magistrates in order to open a new beer-house.

1914: Lloyd George increases beer prices by a halfpenny on the half pint to fund the war effort.

1917: The 18th Amendment to the Constitution (prohibition amendment) is adopted by the required majority of both houses of the American Congress.

1919: The Amendment is ratified. The Volstead Act is passed by Congress.

1920: The Volstead Act takes effect, prohibiting the manufacture, sale, transportation, import and export of intoxicating liquors for beverage purposes.

1920-33: The illicit alcohol trade booms in the United States.

1933: Prohibition is repealed.

1935: Alcoholics Anonymous is established.

1944: The US Public Health Service labels alcoholism the fourth-largest health problem.

1945: The current UK licensing laws are established.

1976: The Scots become the first UK nation to legalize all-day drinking.

1978: Former US first lady Betty Ford admits an addiction to alcohol and drugs.

1989: The UK Monopolies and Mergers Commission inquiry accuses the big six British brewers of unfair practices – they control three-quarters of Britain's pubs between them, and beer prices are rising way ahead of inflation. The government orders them to dispose of 11,000 pubs and allow their pub tenants to sell a guest beer. The result is a widespread collapse in the pub trade.

1989: The Portman Group is set up by the UK's leading drinks manufacturers.

SOURCES AND RECOMMENDED READING:

Anderson, Digby (editor): *Drinking To Your Health, The Allegations And The Evidence* (Social Affairs Unit, 1989)

British Paediatric Association: *Alcohol And The Young* (Royal College of Physicians, 1995)

Cheever, Susan: *Home Before Dark* (Tauris Parke, 2001)

Donnellan, Craig (editor): *Alcohol Abuse* (Independence Educational Publishers, 2001)

Edwards, Griffith: *Alcohol: The Ambiguous Molecule* (Penguin, 2000)

Ettorre, Elizabeth: *Women And Alcohol* (The Women's Press, 1997)

Ferguson, Sheila: *Drink* (Batsford, 1975)

Goodwin, Donald W: *Alcohol And The Writer* (Andrews McMeel, 1988)

Goodwin, Donald W: *Alcoholism* (Oxford University Press, 2000)

Gossop, Michael: *Living With Drugs* (Wildwood House, 1982)

Grice, Trevor and Scott, Tom: *The Great Brain Robbery* (Aurum Press, 1998)

Harrison, B: *Drink And The Victorians* (Faber, 1971)

Healy, Maurice: *Stay Me With Flagons* (Michael Joseph, 1940)

Hyams, Edward: *Dionysus: A Social History Of The Wine Vine* (Sidgwick & Jackson, 1987)

Kanter, Jonathan and Streissguth, Ann: *The Challenge Of Fetal Alcohol Syndrome: Overcoming Secondary Disabilities* (University of Washington Press, 1997)

Khon, Marek: *Narcomania* (Faber & Faber, 1987)

Monti, Peter M (editor): *Adolescents, Alcohol, And Substance Abuse* (Guilford Press, 2001)

Robinson, Jancis: *On The Demon Drink* (Mitchell Beazley, 1988)

Windle, Michael: *Alcohol Use Among Adolescents* (Sage Publications, 1997)

INDEX

Also available
in this series

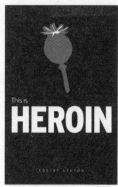